SPIRITUAL FRIENDS

T0057292

SPIRITUAL FRIENDS

MEDITATIONS

BY MONKS AND NUNS *of the*
INTERNATIONAL MAHAYANA INSTITUTE

Edited by Thubten Dondrub

WISDOM PUBLICATIONS • BOSTON

Wisdom Publications, Inc.
199 Elm Street
Somerville MA 02144 USA

www.wisdompubs.org

© 2001 International Mahayana Institute

All rights reserved.

No part of this book may be reproduced in any form or by any means,
electronic or mechanical, including photocopying, recording, or by any
information storage and retrieval system or technologies now known or
later developed, without permission in writing from the publisher.

Library of Congress Cataloging-in-Publication Data
Spiritual friends: meditations / by monks and nuns of the
International Mahayana Institute ; edited by Thubten Dondrob.
        p. cm.
     Includes bibliographical references.
     ISBN 0-86171-325-7
     1. Meditation—Mahayana Buddhism. 2. Spiritual life—
Mahayana Buddhism. 3. Mahayana Buddhism—Doctrines.
4. Monastic and religious life (Buddhism)—United States.
I. Thubten Dondrub, 1947– II. International Mahayana Institute.
BQ9288.S75 2001
294.3'4432—dc21   2001056199

06 05 04 03 02
6   5   4   3   2

Cover calligraphy: Tibetan word for "Sangha,"
by Lama Zopa Rinpoche
Interior line art by Ven. Thubten Norzin (Ingrid Braun)
Designed by Gopa & Ted2

Wisdom Publications' books are printed on acid-free paper and meet the
guidelines for permanence and durability set by the Committee on Production Guidelines for Book Longevity of the Council on Library
Resources.

   Printed in the United States

Table of Contents

The Nuns and Monks

Foreword

THIS MEDITATION BOOK has been compiled by eighteen monks and nuns of the International Mahayana Institute who have been living in ordination for many years, mostly in the Western supermarket of desire. It will prove useful to many readers, both old and new, because the contributors have not just copied the words from the texts, but have meditated extensively upon the topics about which they write. Furthermore, they have not only visualized these meditations but have also tried as hard as they can to integrate the meaning of the words into their lives. Therefore, what they say is neither dry nor empty.

I'm sure this book will inspire many people to turn their backs on the ocean of samsara—the continuity of their five aggregates, the contaminated seeds of disturbing thoughts that form the basis of future suffering—and direct their lives toward liberation and full enlightenment.

My message to readers is: make yourselves strong and be heroic in overcoming the negative emotional thoughts of self-cherishing and the delusions, and please take the opportunity afforded by this precious human life to achieve enlightenment.

Thubten Zopa Rinpoche

Editor's Preface

THIS IS THE FIRST BOOK produced by the International Mahayana Institute (IMI). It owes its origins to Moon Wong, a Chinese Malaysian living in Australia. As a longtime student of Lama Thubten Zopa Rinpoche, Moon wanted a book that would be a tribute to the vital contribution the IMI Sangha have made to the development of the Foundation for the Preservation of the Mahayana Tradition (FPMT). She hoped it would help people to appreciate the importance of establishing the Sangha in the West and the need to support it. For these reasons a short autobiography of each author has been included. All the senior members of the IMI were asked to contribute to the book, but unfortunately some of our most senior members were unable to, for the very reason that so much of their time is already taken up with their FPMT commitments.

Each of the eighteen contributors to this book was asked to write on any topic from the Graduated Path (Lamrim), presenting it from their own perspective, drawing from their own experience of what works in meditation. There has been some overlap in themes covered, but rather than being repetitive, this provides the reader with alternative perspectives for contemplation. The book is meant to be a practical meditation manual that can be taken anywhere and used on a daily basis. We have tried to make the meditations accessible both to beginners trying to find a meaningful system of meditation to practice, and to committed Buddhist practitioners.

Our true spiritual friends are our mind's positive potentials, which will never disappoint us and never desert us. Similarly, the teachings and meditations that enable us to develop those potentials are true friends to whom we can always turn. Likewise, the Sangha, as the ordained followers of the Buddha upon whom the continued existence of the Buddha's teachings depend, are spiritual friends who encourage us and inspire us to transform our minds. Their presence among us reminds us of the Buddha and of our own potential for enlightenment—our buddha nature.

The International Mahayana Institute is extremely grateful to Moon Wong for developing the idea for this book and sponsoring it. Moreover, we have appreciated her gentle and patient encouragement over the long period it has taken to produce this book. It simply would not have happened without her. The IMI would also like to thank the many individuals and centers who helped financially by offering free e-mail access, telephone calls, postage, and so forth.

I wish to thank all the monks and nuns who contributed to this book. The FPMT has a presence in twenty-five countries around the world. IMI Sangha are represented in fourteen of these countries. The eighteen authors in this book come from six of these countries. I also wish to thank the many people who helped bring this book to completion. I am especially grateful to Nick Ribush for various bits of advice and for kindly supplying some material from the Lama Yeshe Wisdom Archives books; Ven. Pende of Nalanda Monastery and Ven. Holly Ansett (Tenzin Chimme) for patiently e-mailing material; Ven. Bertrand Cayla (Jampa Legmoen) and Nick Dawson for scanning photos; Ven. Losang Dolma (S. Angela Bleackley) for keying-in and scanning some material; Ven. Ingrid (Thubten Norzin) for the line drawings of monks and nuns, for the decorative motifs, and for drawing the IMI logo based on a design by Lama Thubten Zopa Rinpoche; and Ven. Tenzin Chime (Barbara Gilman) for editing some of the material. Thanks also to Donath-Karl Pirs for taking photos of Ven. Angeles de la Torre and myself, to Pearl Bailey for her photo of Ven. Fedor, to Debbie Yazbek of *The Star* for the photo of Ven. Chantal, to Mark Gatter for his help with production, and to the staff of Wisdom Publications for their help in making this book a reality.

Most particularly I would like to thank Ven. Angeles de la Torre and members of Nagarjuna Centro–Alicante, Spain for allowing me to stay at their center for a month to complete the book and for helping out in many ways; and Ven. Losang Yeshe (Tom Szymanski) for checking and improving the whole text. I cannot thank all these people enough.

Whatever merit has been created or will be created in relation to this book, may it become the cause for all beings to quickly develop a peaceful mind free of any thought to harm. May we develop perfect refuge in the Three Jewels and the gurus who embody their sublime qualities.

Because of this may we quickly achieve liberation and complete enlightenment.

In particular, may this book inspire others to follow the ordained way of life and to do so purely without pride. In this way, may more and more people develop faith in the Buddha's Sangha and support their practice so that the Buddha's teachings spread and flourish everywhere.

By the merit of sponsoring this book, may Moon Wong have a long and healthy life and experience the fulfillment of all her Dharma wishes. May her deceased parents always find perfect conditions to practice the Dharma, be immediately freed from all suffering, and quickly achieve enlightenment.

May the dependent arising of this book please the holy minds of our gurus: His Holiness the Dalai Lama, Lama Thubten Zopa Rinpoche, Lama Thubten Yeshe, and his incarnation, Lama Tenzin Osel Rinpoche. May it be a cause for them to live long and healthy lives, effortlessly accomplishing all that they wish.

None of the monks and nuns in this book lay claim to any special status as spiritual guides, but simply by taking ordination vows a person is placed in the role of being a spiritual friend to all people. This is both humbling and inspiring. I think it is the wish of every member of the IMI to become a genuine spiritual friend to all who need one.

I hope you find in this book a true spiritual friend for these confused and troubled times in which we all live.

Thubten Dondrub
Nalanda Monastery
Lavaur, France
March 2001

Introduction

WHETHER WE ARE AWARE of it or not, everything we do in life is motivated by the wish to experience happiness—however we define it—and to avoid discomfort, pain, and problems. Most of us, most of the time, try to achieve these results by relying on a whole range of things that are external to us—friends and family, wealth and possessions, reputation, power, influence, and so on. With a minimum of intelligence and time, however, it is possible to recognize that everything we depend on for happiness is not really dependable at all. Why? Simply because none of it can last. Is there anything that *does* last, that we can depend on to bring freedom from suffering and genuine, lasting peace? According to the Buddha, there is. He showed that we can rely on our own minds. To do that we need to discover the true nature of the mind and work with it in a skillful and compassionate way. This is learned through meditation.

One especially useful method of mental training was developed by Lama Atisha in the eleventh century and brought to perfection by Lama Tsongkhapa, the founder of the Gelug school of Tibetan Buddhism. This system, called the Graduated Path (Lamrim), is designed to lead the mind away from confusion, self-obsession, and suffering toward inner peace, perfect insight into one's own true nature, and the compassionate ability to genuinely benefit others. The Graduated Path contains the essence of all the Buddha's teachings arranged in a progressive, psychological way that ordinary people can readily understand and practice.

The purpose of the meditations in this book is not simply to bring about some temporary benefit in this life. If done correctly and regularly they will lead to a radical transformation of one's mind away from thinking of just this life, just oneself, and just worldly pleasure and comfort. The final result of this training is to achieve enlightenment where the full potential of one's mind is fully active and fully manifest in a way that brings everlasting peace and satisfaction to oneself and only benefits all other beings.

Those unfamiliar with Buddhism and with this particular Tibetan approach to analytical meditation will find some explanation of terms in the glossary and can refer to the "Further Reading" section for books that can clarify unfamiliar ideas and practices. It is ideal to receive teachings on the Graduated Path from qualified masters. Then one is really blessed with the right foundations to meditate successfully.

✦ HOW TO USE THIS BOOK ✦

To get the most out of these meditations, the masters of the past developed a procedure that first prepares the body and mind to do the meditation, keeps the mind on the meditation topic, and brings the meditation to a satisfactory conclusion. The present Tibetan masters, such as Lama Thubten Zopa Rinpoche, who uphold this old but vibrant tradition, stress again and again how important it is to do the preliminary practices—especially generating the right motivation—to ensure the best result from our meditations and so that they become truly transforming spiritual practices. They are the keys to success in using meditation to free the mind of suffering and liberate its genuine nature of compassion, wisdom, and joy. Having made this effort to benefit oneself and others, we then conclude our meditation by dedicating the merit. This way all that good effort is not lost.

A brief version of the essential points of this traditional meditation procedure is presented in the next chapter, called "Meditation Session Outline." You may wish to incorporate some or all of these elements into the meditations that follow. For this reason each meditation includes these three sections: preliminaries, the meditation, and dedication. Since the authors were given complete freedom as to how to write their meditations, some have provided preliminaries and dedications while others have not. Where these instructions are not given, the reader can refer to the "Meditation Session Outline" to learn how to do them. Traditional motivation prayers that you may wish to incorporate have also been included. Even where the author has suggested some preliminaries or a dedication, these can be supplemented by the ones in the "Meditation Session Outline."

✦ THE PARTS OF THE MEDITATION SESSION ✦

Preliminaries

When embarking on a long, arduous journey, it is wise to be not just healthy but really fit and strong as well. When meditating to transform the mind from dissatisfaction to liberation and enlightenment, it is also wise to not rely only on our ordinary worldly mind. We need to purify our mind of all sorts of negative imprints to make our mind really healthy and, at the same time, we need to empower our mind by building up a store of positive energy. Using such a mind, meditation then becomes the key to bring about definite, stable, and lasting transformation, or realization. Using our ordinary mind, meditation is often just a disappointing struggle.

The preliminary practices are mainly for the purpose of purifying the mind and building up virtuous potentials. These potentials will make it easier to understand the purpose and content of the meditation; easier to keep concentrated on the content of the meditation; easier to do the meditation with the right motivation; and, consequently, easier to develop some real insight and transformation.

The Meditation

The order of the meditations in this book generally follows the outline of the Graduated Path, although not all the topics are covered. The Graduated Path can be considered from the point of view of developing the three principal qualities of renunciation, bodhichitta, and wisdom.

Another way of classifying the Graduated Path is from the point of view of the three scopes, which refers to the scope, or level of capability, of the practitioner's mind. Upon entering the spiritual path we train in the small scope, which involves developing the basic level of renunciation—giving up our obsession with the illusory happiness of this life.

Then we can advance to the middle scope, where we develop complete renunciation of cyclic existence and the determination to achieve liberation from all suffering. In the highest, or great scope, we are able to train in bodhichitta, the mind that seeks not just liberation for only oneself but complete enlightenment in order to perfectly benefit each and every sentient being.

The first meditation in the book outlines all three scopes; the next three meditations cover aspects of training in the small scope. Meditations five, six, and seven are related to the middle scope, while all the remaining meditations are part of the great scope. The last four meditations in the book are loosely related to the wisdom aspect of the great scope.

You will discover after using these meditations, as with studying the complete Graduated Path teachings, that familiarity with one topic gives more understanding of the others; they are all part of an organic whole. A simple example is in the Venerable Gyatso's meditation on loving-kindness, where he suggests doing a preliminary meditation on the clarity of the mind. Later in the book is a complete meditation on this topic by the Venerable Tsultrim.

Our teachers stress that we need to do these meditations again and again in order to train our minds. Through the power of familiarity our minds become accustomed to these new ways of thinking and perceiving, and transformation occurs. We need to be prepared to do this for our entire lives. One way is to work through the book step by step, doing a different meditation each day. So after eighteen days you start again at the beginning. Or you can concentrate on each meditation for a week or a month and then move on to the next one. It is useful to read a brief outline of the entire Graduated Path at the beginning of each meditation to familiarize yourself with the path and to help give a sense of how the particular meditation you are about to do fits into the path to enlightenment. A very beautiful Lamrim prayer translated by Lama Zopa Rinpoche has been included in the "Meditation Session Outline" for this purpose.

Some of the meditations present instructions that are easy to follow. Some ask us to "check up," while others are presented more from the point of view of an established faith in the teachings. The latter simply state Dharma points with the aim of allowing them to become more integrated with our minds. But even here meditators—especially those who are new—can, and should, question these statements; that is what meditation or contemplation is about. As Lama Yeshe used to say: "Check up!"

Also don't just use the points in the book; you may see other connections that haven't been developed in the meditation. Each meditation is meant to be fleshed out with your own experience and understanding. Like all Lamrim teachings, these meditations merely form a framework within which to develop your own reflections.

Each meditation has been set out so that the paragraph breaks indicate where one should spend time contemplating the meaning before going on to the next one. As mentioned, this can involve active questioning, debating the validity and applicability of the point, or it may mean a calm reflection on it. For those new to these meditation subjects, many of the points may bring up questions, but with repeated meditation over some months on these, there may be fewer questions and more accepting reflection on them. With more time and experience, a whole new set of deeper questions may arise. Lama Yeshe described meditation as an active, alert confrontation with reality.

Conclusion

Some of the meditations finish with a conclusion. Even if they don't, it is good to make one suitable to the topic of that meditation. One aspect of the conclusion that applies to all meditations is to make the decision to be more mindful in daily life of what you have meditated on, in order to practice it whenever it is appropriate.

Dedication

Some authors have supplied a dedication, while others have not; so again the reader can refer to the "Meditation Session Outline" for what to do to conclude the session and for the traditional prayers to dedicate the merit.

✦ POSTURE ✦

Sitting correctly is very important. If you are new to meditation, it is worthwhile to put a lot of time and effort into learning how to sit properly. The perfect posture is called the seven-point posture of Vairochana. If done completely, it involves sitting in the cross-legged full-lotus position. This element is only crucial for advanced stages of meditation, but the other aspects are helpful from the beginning; especially proper positioning of the spine. It doesn't matter whether you sit on a cushion or in a chair, but don't lean against the wall or the back of the chair.

✦ DEALING WITH ✦
DULLNESS AND DISTRACTION

There are two main types of meditation: analytical meditation, which focuses on developing insight, and stabilizing meditation, which focuses on improving concentration. Even though all the meditations in this book are of the analytic type, concentration is still needed. We have to keep our minds on the topic at hand. The mind may become bored, dull, sleepy, or agitated. All these mental states are distractions that interfere with developing liberating insight and virtuous states of mind.

Just a few points can be mentioned in relation to this huge topic. There are three main types of distractions: sounds, pain in the body, and irrelevant thoughts. Regarding sounds or pains in our body, we cannot stop them, but we can choose whether or not to pay attention to them. What helps us to not pay attention is the strength and purity of our motivation and our determination.

Regarding irrelevant thoughts, some kinds of meditation focus on reducing conceptual activity. During Lamrim meditation, however, we are trying to generate wise, virtuous thoughts, and to analyze logically what is and what is not true and beneficial. Thoughts such as these are not obstacles at all and are not considered irrelevant. But all unwise, nonvirtuous thoughts are. These too can be overcome to some extent by the strength of our motivation and determination, but specific antidotes may be required. When the mind becomes dull or depressed, it is important to lift it up. This can be done by visualizing very bright light or by thinking on a virtuous subject that makes the mind happy, such as one's buddha nature. When the dullness dissipates, go back to the original meditation topic. When the mind becomes agitated, especially by some aspect of attachment, it is helpful to think of something to bring the mind down a little, such as impermanence or death.

Another method is simply to see whatever thought arises as just that—it is only a thought. If we get caught up in it and feed it, the thought takes over our mind; but if we simply note its arising, label it "distraction," and not buy into it, then it will fade away. We have to use mindfulness to be aware of what is going on in our mind as we meditate, and when we note that dullness or agitation is starting to arise, we have to do something about it. Developing mindfulness in order to quickly notice distractions and then skillfully applying the correct antidote, or the antidote that works best for us, is the key to meaningful and effective meditation.

❖

Finally, perform the meditations in the spirit of no expectation. It doesn't matter if you feel that the meditation goes well or not, that no particular changes seem to take place during or after the meditation. The main thing is to do it—have faith in your own buddha nature and faith in the Buddhist path—and keep doing it. One great Tibetan master emphasized we should not expect results in this life, but have confidence that by practicing we are making very strong imprints that will definitely benefit us in future lives.

A Meditation Session Outline

✦ **PRELIMINARIES** ✦

The place. The tradition is to meditate in a place set aside for that purpose; have an altar with at least an image of the Buddha; make offerings such as incense, light, flowers, and pure water; keep that area very clean.

Prostrations. Before sitting down to meditate it is good to make three prostrations to the Three Jewels.

Posture. Sit in a comfortable position, with your spine straight and shoulders perpendicular to it. Your arms should be slightly away from your body, your hands resting relaxed on your lap with the right hand on top of the left and the thumbs lightly touching. Let your head tilt slightly forward with your chin slightly tucked in. Your mouth should be in a natural position, your tongue resting at the palate, touching the back of the upper teeth. You will need to read the sections of the meditation, but apart from this, keep your eyes just a little bit open while contemplating each part. Try to gaze, in an unfocused way, at a point no more than an arm's length away. This is not easy at first, but in the long run it is very effective. If you find it too difficult, then keep the eyes lightly closed. You can spend a few minutes going through the body from head to feet becoming aware of tension. Just your awareness of the tension can help loosen it.

Breathing Meditation. Begin to bring your mind inward, away from all external stimulation. Have an attitude of contentment with sitting quietly, not wanting to do anything else or be anywhere else. Without force or expectation we are trying to create the conditions for the mind to become more calm and clear, to reveal its natural state. Focus on the natural rhythm of your breathing. Don't change it, just observe it. There are two breathing meditations you can use preliminary to doing analytical meditation. One is the nine-round breathing exercise, the other is counting the breath.

NINE-ROUND BREATHING EXERCISE. As you breathe normally through both nostrils, observe the sensation at the tip of the nostrils caused by the breath as it comes and goes. First focus on this sensation as the breath comes in the right nostril and leaves from the left nostril. Do this for three successive breaths. Then focus on the sensation as it comes in the left nostril and leaves through the right nostril. Do this for three successive breaths. Then focus on the sensation as it comes in both nostrils and leaves both nostrils for three successive breaths. This completes one cycle. This exercise can be done for three cycles. A variation on this exercise is to visualize, as you focus on the in-breaths, blissful white light—symbolizing all the perfect qualities of the buddhas—coming in and filling the whole body and mind. Then, as you focus on the out-breaths, visualize all agitation, distraction, and negative thoughts in the form of inky black liquid, leaving your body and completely disappearing.

COUNTING THE BREATH. As above, this involves noting the sensation at the nostrils as the breath comes and goes. You concentrate on the breath coming and going from both nostrils. As a cycle of one in-breath and out-breath is completed, you count "one" silently. With the next cycle you count "two." In this way try to observe twenty-one successive cycles of the breath. If the mind is distracted from the breath, you should start again from the beginning.

Refuge and motivation. By doing these simple breathing meditations, the mind becomes quieter and is said to be in a neutral state. Now we need to generate a very strong virtuous motivation to ensure the meditation becomes a genuine cause for spiritual growth rather than just a temporary exercise for relaxation, which will have no lasting effect.

The best motivation is the wish to become free of all faults and develop our buddha nature completely so that we can become buddhas to perfectly benefit all living beings. This bodhichitta motivation depends on refuge in the Buddha, Dharma, and Sangha—the Three Jewels.

For this reason we visualize in the clear space in front of us, an arm's length away and at the height of our forehead, Shakyamuni Buddha. Try to imagine the Buddha surrounded by many other buddhas, bodhisattvas, and holy beings. Visualize all beings living in the universe sitting together with you. You can imagine your mother on your left and your father on your right; your friends and relatives behind you; and the people you do not get along with very well in front of you. Surrounding you are all other beings of the six realms of samsara. Imagine them in human form, but experiencing the sufferings unique to each realm. Think:

"The teachings have their immaculate source in the Buddha himself and are designed to free all beings from lower rebirths, cyclic existence, and lead them to liberation and enlightenment. Many followers of the Buddha have realized the direct antidote to afflictions and can provide unmistaken assistance. However, it is only by obtaining the supreme state of a buddha that one has the perfect wisdom, compassion, and ability to lead all beings without exception out of suffering. I, too, can attain that state, and I must do so in order to bring about the liberation and enlightenment of all beings."

Then recite the prayer of going for refuge and generating bodhichitta:

To the Buddha, Dharma, and Sangha,
I go for refuge until enlightenment.
By the merit from giving and other perfections,
may I achieve buddhahood to benefit all.

Offerings. Then to purify the mind and create merit you can do the seven-limb prayer:

I prostrate with my body, speech, and mind in faith
and make each and every offering, both actually arranged and
    mentally transformed.

I confess all transgressions and negativities committed since
   beginningless time
and rejoice in the virtues of ordinary beings and aryas.
Please remain until cyclic existence is emptied
and turn the wheel of Dharma for the sake of migrators.
I dedicate the merits of myself and others to the great enlightenment.

And then make a mandala offering where you visualize offering the
entire universe to the buddhas:

This ground anointed with perfume, strewn with flowers,
adorned with Mt. Meru, four continents, sun and moon,
I offer visualized as buddha fields.
May all sentient beings enjoy these pure lands.

Requests and purification visualization. Make a strong request to your
teacher (who should be seen as one with Shakyamuni Buddha), and to
all the buddhas, bodhisattvas, and other holy beings to bless your mind
to be able to do the meditation correctly. Make a strong determination not to be distracted during the meditation but to do it as well as
one can.

Imagine that Shakyamuni Buddha is extremely pleased. Light and
nectar stream from his brow, throat, and heart chakras and enter one's
own brow, throat, and heart chakras. They purify all negativities—
especially those blocking understanding and realization of the particular meditation you are about to do—and grant blessings to receive all
the realizations of the path, particularly of this meditation.

Now it is useful to read through an outline of the whole Graduated
Path to enlightenment to understand where the meditation you are
about to do fits into the path. This also makes a strong imprint of the
whole path in the mind. The following prayer is very suitable:

Refuge

I take refuge in the holy guru, essence of all buddhas, original
grantor of all holy teachings, and lord of all supreme beings.

Prayer for success in Dharma practice
Please all guru-buddhas, bestow on me the ability to unify my mind with the Dharma and to be successful in practicing Dharma to accomplish the Graduated Path. May no hindrances occur while achieving this path.

Prayer of the practitioner of small scope
Please bless me to realize I have received a perfect human rebirth, highly meaningful, difficult to obtain, transient, fragile, and—due to its changeable nature—decaying in the shortest moment. Thus my death is definite but its actual time is most indefinite. After death I am far more likely to be reborn in the lower suffering realms due to having created infinitely more negative than positive karma in this life and all previous lives.

Please bless me to comprehend how incredibly unendurable are the sufferings of the lower realms so that I might take refuge in Buddha, Dharma, and Sangha with all my heart. Bless me to realize the evolution of karma in all its profundity, that I might perform only virtuous actions and abandon all negative actions.

Prayer of the practitioner of middle scope
By practicing in this way I will be reborn in the upper realms, but because of uncontrolled delusion and karma I will still have to experience unlimited suffering. Please bestow upon me the ability to realize fully the evolution of samsara, from uncontrolled rebirth to death to rebirth, and to be able to follow, day and night, the three higher practices of the path: higher conduct, concentration, and wisdom, the main methods to release me from samsara.

The prayer of the practitioner of the great scope
THE SUTRAYANA PATH: Each sentient being has been my mother, and most of them are in extreme suffering. Please bless me to bring success to all of them by renouncing the perfect happiness of self, and by practicing the bodhisattva's deeds of

the six perfections with a mind of exchanging self with others, on the basis of the equanimity meditation.

Having trained my mind in the general path I shall have no sorrow in experiencing the sufferings of all other sentient beings, no matter how long.

THE VAJRAYANA PATH: Please bless me to be able to follow the quick Vajrayana teachings, by feeling sentient beings' suffering—unimaginably unbearable for even the shortest moment—as my own. Bless me to be able to achieve the attainments of Guru Shakyamuni immediately, at this very moment, by keeping with the greatest care my ordination and the instructions of the guru. For these reasons I shall meditate on the Graduated Path to enlightenment.

✦ THE MEDITATION ✦

✦ CONCLUSION ✦

Make the decision to be more mindful in daily life of what you have meditated on, in order to practice it whenever it is appropriate.

Then visualize that the field of merit from the beginning of the meditation all dissolves into Shakyamuni Buddha, who then comes to the crown of your head, dissolves into brilliant golden light, which streams down into you. Concentrate on feeling that the Buddha's mind and your mind have become inseparably one and that you have been blessed to receive the realization of the meaning of the meditation.

✦ DEDICATION ✦

Now dedicate the merit, or positive potential, that has been created in the mind, so that it ripens not as some ordinary form of happiness, but as a cause for the peerless state of enlightenment that enables you to benefit all suffering mother sentient beings.

May the precious bodhi mind
not yet born arise and grow.
May that born have no decline
but increase forever more.

By this virtue may I quickly
attain the state of a guru-buddha
to lead all living beings without exception
into that enlightened state.

Just as Manjushri and Samantabhadra
have realized things as they are,
I dedicate this virtue in the best way,
that I too may follow after them.

I dedicate all these roots of virtue
To the sublime bodhisattva conduct
with the same dedication praised as best
by the three times' conquerors gone to bliss.

THE MEDITATIONS

A Meditation on the Three Scopes

Tenzin Tsapel (Gillian Jelbart)

✦ PRELIMINARIES ✦

Visualize the refuge field with Shakyamuni Buddha in the center surrounded by all the buddhas and bodhisattvas. Think that each one embodies every holy object and is one in essence with one's own guru.

Think:
The bases for Buddha's achievements were the body and mind of an ordinary being just like me. Every moment of my present life is extremely useful. Each day, hour, minute, and second I can purify so much negative karma and produce so many causes for good rebirths until I achieve enlightenment. How can I actually take the essence of my perfect human rebirth?

I must avoid craving the pleasure, material wealth, praise, and fame of this life for myself alone; and must avoid craving to be free of pain, loss, criticism, or bad reputation. Actions influenced by these intentions cannot bring about any happiness or higher goal.

I must accept without craving or aversion whatever difficult, neutral, or happy state arises and use whatever experience I have to train my mind in the three scopes.

✦ THE MEDITATION ✦

By training in the path shared with the small scope, I can develop a strong yearning for a happy rebirth, followed by enthusiastic effort to study and train in the means to obtain it. Yearning for a happy rebirth requires understanding that my life is short and I will soon die.

There are many drawbacks from not remembering death and many advantages to my practice if I do. Death is inevitable, its time is uncertain, and nothing but Dharma will help at the time of death. By meditating on the aspects of the actual death process I can learn to use my life and death to progress on the path.

Yearning for a happy rebirth also requires fear of the very real and extensive sufferings of lower rebirths as a hell being, a hungry ghost, or an animal. Naturally, I long for a happy rebirth with the freedoms and endowments to continue my spiritual path.

To obtain a happy rebirth I need heartfelt refuge in the supreme physician, the Buddha; the medicine of Dharma; and the assistants, the realized Sangha. This comes from: seeing myself as a patient, fear of the unfortunate states, and faith in the Three Jewels as both perfect guides and the cure.

To obtain a happy rebirth I need to develop faith in cause and effect, the root of all happiness. Any physical, verbal, or mental action has a result that can only be concordant with the motivating intention, and that result will greatly increase. This is as definite as a mango seed giving rise to only a mango tree. Being fearful of the results, I must abandon and purify negative actions as I would poison. I should accumulate only virtue and rejoice in all virtue, knowing only a good result will come.

By training in the path shared with the middle scope I can develop a strong yearning for liberation from the contaminated states within cyclic existence. This will be followed by enthusiastic effort to study and train in the means to obtain the peace of nirvana, free of the delusions and their seeds.

I need to understand that wherever I take rebirth within cyclic existence, I will never be free from suffering. Any happiness does not last long and is followed by suffering, like the revolving of a Ferris wheel. I must find a way to be free.

To ascertain the path to liberation I must understand that the origin of all suffering is the afflictions—attachment, anger, pride, ignorance, doubt, and deluded views—and the karmic seeds produced by them. I am bound to the wheel of suffering by ignorance, craving, and grasping. I need to cut that rope with ethics, concentration, and the direct antidote to the root of delusions, wisdom realizing selflessness.

By training in the great scope stages of the path, I can develop heartfelt concern for all and the mind of bodhichitta—the strong resolve to free all beings without exception from the cycle of suffering and wishing to obtain buddhahood in order to do just that. This training is based on first training in the previous two scopes.

Genuine bodhichitta is the entry to the Mahayana path. It will accomplish all my wishes, easily purify all my obstacles, accumulate enormous merit, and quickly enable me to complete all the stages of the path. Knowing these extensive benefits, I should enthusiastically aspire to develop bodhichitta.

First I have to develop a feeling of equanimity toward strangers, enemies, and friends. Whether they help or harm, all others are just like myself, wanting happiness and not wanting mental or physical discomfort. But kept hostage by afflictions, they continuously meet with suffering, and happiness is either hard to find or passes quickly. In the past I have been born impoverished and helpless infinite times to none other than the countless strangers, enemies, and friends around me now. They raised me with so much kindness, but with each successive rebirth I have lost contact with them. Like my dear ones now, all of them have been kind beyond measure. May they dwell in true peace and happiness, free of suffering and its causes. I must bring that about. I must attain the supreme state of buddhahood to be able to do this.

To develop and strengthen my bodhichitta resolve, I should take the bodhisattva vows, through purification keep them from degenerating, and retake them when necessary. I must never separate from bodhichitta and must always practice the bodhisattva perfections of generosity, ethics, patience, perseverance, calm abiding, and wisdom. Wisdom comes from combining calm abiding with special insight focused on emptiness. This wisdom is the ultimate bodhichitta, the antidote that uproots the obscurations to liberation and knowledge and brings about perfect buddhahood.

Visualize the field of refuge dissolving into the central figure of Shakyamuni Buddha. He then comes to the crown of your head and dissolves into brilliant golden light, which streams down through your crown chakra and completely dissolves into your heart, bringing blessings to realize the three scopes in your mindstream.

✦ DEDICATION ✦

A Meditation on Guru Devotion and the Precious Human Rebirth

Jampa Shenphen (Jesus Revert)

✦ INTRODUCTION ✦

I do this meditation in the morning; it helps to point the mind in a good direction, and it strengthens mindfulness and enthusiasm for practice for the rest of the day. It is very helpful at the beginning of a retreat or as a motivation for the daily practice of a sadhana.

The meditation should be done until a mind of joy for having the opportunity to practice Dharma and the wish to practice bodhichitta appears clearly and genuinely. In the beginning it may take some time and much reasoning, but with familiarity it will appear without much effort.

If this motivation is sincerely generated—at the beginning of a session, in a daily practice, during a retreat, or for any other Dharma activity—the whole practice will go much better, and there will be fewer obstacles and distractions. Like any other Dharma practice for beginners like us, it requires some effort and continuity, but, later on, once we become familiar with it, it becomes much easier and it brings so many benefits in all aspects of our life.

Personally, I find this meditation very helpful, especially when doing retreat, daily meditations, or when taking the eight Mahayana precepts. I hope it may also be beneficial for others.

✦ PRELIMINARIES ✦

✦ THE MEDITATION ✦

In the past, haven't I often been anxious and worried about my problems and the meaning of life; full of doubts, uncertainty; feeling unsatisfied and without hope for the future?

Haven't I wasted a good part of my life with meaningless distractions?

Haven't I now found the precious way of the Buddhadharma?

These teachings show clearly the reality of life and its causes and conditions. They reveal life's true meaning and the path leading to the full accomplishment of this great meaning. Haven't I met a teacher who himself has complete experience of the path to enlightenment?

Doesn't he show me and others, with love and kindness, how to practice the path?

Only he can explain the teachings of Buddha in a way that fits my mind, and he shows with his own example how to practice the Dharma and how to enjoy its fruits. Apart from his teachings there is no other way I can know what a Buddha is or how to follow the Buddhist path.

Because of the infinite kindness of my precious guru—the essence of all buddhas—I have right now all the conditions to practice Dharma perfectly and to eliminate all my sufferings and problems. In this life and in countless past lives I have been a slave to my ignorance and other delusions, without any chance of escaping. But right now, I have the ideal situation to achieve all I have been looking for in the past.

I have met a precious teacher who knows the path to enlightenment and who has followed that path himself and has achieved its fruit.

I have received his teachings and instructions about what should be put into practice and how to practice it, what should be avoided and how to avoid it.

Unlike other sentient beings who are in unfortunate circumstances—hell-beings, hungry ghosts, or animals; those born in places of war, famine, or misery; those without any intelligence, living in places where Dharma does not exist, or believing in wrong views—I am now free of all those hindrances.

This perfect situation I have right now will not last long. It may last for a few months, a few days, only one day, or just one hour. Very soon I will be completely involved in all kinds of worldly affairs without any chance to practice Dharma even if I very strongly wish for it.

So many times in the past I wished, hoped, and prayed to find the perfect conditions I am enjoying now. Having this situation is the fruit of much effort, virtue, and many prayers previously done for it.

This perfect situation to practice Dharma that I am enjoying now is extremely rare and is difficult to obtain. I can see this very clearly by looking at my own life or at the lives of others. Many people in the world would give all they have to be able to enjoy the practice of Dharma as I do now.

At this very moment, there are so many people experiencing all kinds of painful circumstances: being completely depressed and confused; feeling sad, lonely, and hopeless; painfully facing the horrors of sickness, old age, and death. They would do anything to change their situations for the one I have now. In a short while, I may come to be like them, so I must not waste even one second.

Life goes by so quickly, day after day, month after month, and I am constantly caught up in daily affairs and problems. But suddenly it will come to an end, and then I will find only anguish and regret, seeing that all the worldly things I have been doing and working for will only be lost and of no benefit at all.

If I let my mind follow the distractions of thinking about the past or planning for the future, complain about small and meaningless discomforts, or indulge in selfish pleasures, then that would be a terrible waste of this most precious time that is so difficult to find and so easily lost.

I received the bodhichitta instructions from my guru, and, in front of him, I made the promise to work for the happiness of all sentient beings by achieving enlightenment for their sake. Having promised that, it would be the most shameful cheating of my precious guru and of all sentient beings if now I waste this opportunity by letting my mind follow worldly distractions. This would be the cause of endless pain and the loss of a unique opportunity.

By remembering that, and by feeling great joy for having these wonderful conditions due to the infinite kindness of my precious teacher, I am going to take the essence of this perfect human rebirth. Today I am going to do my Dharma practice with strong mindfulness from the beginning, through the middle, and to the end. I am going to keep constant alertness and avoid distractions even before they appear. I am going to practice Bodhichitta with joy and mindfulness in all my actions of body, speech, and mind. This will be the best offering to my guru who is the essence of all Buddhas. This will be the best way of giving happiness and of pacifying the sufferings of all sentient beings. This will be the best way to solve my problems and dispel all my fears.

✦ DEDICATION ✦

A Meditation on the Lower Realms

Yeshe Choedzom (Margaret McAndrew)

✦ INTRODUCTION ✦

This meditation is traditionally presented as part of the small scope section of the Graduated Path. It follows from meditating on death and impermanence and is done in order to strengthen our motivation for taking refuge and practicing Dharma. Its purpose is not to terrify us but to help us take the means of gaining happy rebirths as human beings into our own hands and thereby be able to progress to liberation and enlightenment.

Some people may have difficulty accepting some of these rebirth states, but we should not dismiss them without contemplation and investigation. It is helpful to remember that all our rebirth states, including this human one, are karmicly created and illusory.

There are six realms of samsara: the three upper realms of the gods, demi-gods, and human beings are happy rebirths, the results of good karma. The three lower realms of animals, pretas (hungry spirits), and narak (hell) beings are suffering rebirths. There are many karmic causes for rebirth in each of these realms. In general, rebirth in the naraks is the result of the worst karma, the pretas of lighter negative karma, and animal rebirths the result of the lightest negative karmas.

If you have difficulty accepting the literal reality of some of these realms, don't worry. The essential point is to feel convinced that we do have past and future lives; and in our future lives we will experience the karmic results of our present actions; and, for very harmful actions, the result could be a lifetime of extreme suffering. We can also see situations where human beings experience sufferings similar to those of animals, pretas, and hell beings.

Great practitioners of the past have found these contemplations extremely valuable, and not all of these practitioners have been Buddhists. Saint Teresa of Avila, for example, had many blissful visions but once had a vision of hell. Afterward she said this was her best vision because of the stimulus it gave to her practice.

In this meditation we need to use our imagination and visualize ourselves experiencing these sufferings. By this we generate strong renunciation of samsara and energy for Dharma practice, and in this way, by thinking how other beings are suffering, we also develop compassion.

✦ PRELIMINARIES ✦

✦ THE MEDITATION ✦

Think: During the course of my beginningless lives I have been born again and again in all the six realms of samsara and especially, due to wrong actions, in the three lower realms. Now I am going to meditate on the sufferings of these realms in order to motivate myself to avoid creating negative actions, and thereby avoid having to experience these sufferings again and again in the future.

The suffering of animals

Imagine that at the end of this life your mind reincarnates in the animal realm, which includes birds, fish, insects, and so forth.

Imagine the suffering of having such a limited body and mind. Like humans they suffer hunger, thirst, heat, and cold, but to a greater degree and with less ability to affect these states. Wild animals are constantly in fear of being killed; domestic animals are exploited and slaughtered. While experiencing so much suffering as an animal, I would mostly create the causes of more suffering.

Apart from this gross suffering, imagine the subtle suffering that exists because of not being able to meet, understand, or practice Dharma.

Animals are under the control of ignorance and—although they possess buddha nature—as animals, they have no capacity to learn about Dharma and cannot act to create the causes for a human rebirth.

Determine to avoid its causes: From now on I will avoid disrespecting Dharma and teachers; lying and gossiping; breaking precepts; killing animals; and calling others, especially Dharma practitioners, by animal names.

The suffering of the pretas

Imagine that at the end of this life your mind incarnates as a preta, or hungry ghost.

Imagine: My mind is completely dominated by craving, but I never find the object I desire. Or if I find it, there is no way I can have it—it is always beyond my reach. I am tormented by unrequited desires—especially for food and drink.

Although weakened by hunger and thirst, I do not die from these conditions but I go on suffering. I am always searching for food and drink but seldom find it. I can only eat dirty and disgusting things that cause burning pain in my body.

The weather is always either extremely hot or extremely cold. I have an extremely ugly, thin, and weak body, and to move my limbs is very painful. The whole environment appears like a vast barren desert. There is no beauty, only harshness.

Although I have some intelligence, because of my suffering and miserliness, it is almost impossible for me to perform any good actions.

Determine to avoid creating the causes: "From now on I will avoid miserliness, covetousness, stealing, and so forth."

The suffering of the hells

Imagine that at the end of this life your mind reincarnates in the hell realms. Whatever we think of as a hellish experience can be used as an example of extreme suffering to give us some idea of these rebirth states.

Imagine: I experience the intense suffering of being completely dominated by my own anger; no other thoughts arise in my mind.

The environment is totally claustrophobic. In the hot hells everything I see, hear, smell, or touch is ugly and repellent. I am surrounded only by frightening and hateful beings who harm me in countless brutal ways. There is also the constant suffering of intense heat.

Some of the sufferings of the hot naraks are: being trapped in burning houses, being crushed between mountains, being tortured by karmicly created hell guards, or being forced to fight battles on a ground of red-hot iron, and to kill and be killed over and over again.

In the cold hells I am completely alone with my angry mind. I am trapped in ice, totally frozen by my cold indifference to the suffering of others; I am imprisoned in utter darkness.

How could I possibly practice any kind of virtue in such a situation? I would have no possibility of practicing Dharma.

Make a strong determination: "I will avoid creating the causes for such a rebirth—killing or harming any sentient being, particularly through strong anger and hatred.

✦ CONCLUSION ✦

Instead of sending myself to these suffering realms in the future, I must use this precious human rebirth to practice Dharma in order to create the causes for further precious human rebirths and to progress toward liberation and enlightenment.

✦ DEDICATION ✦

A Meditation on Impermanence and Death

Thubten Dondrub (Neil Huston)

Thinking about impermanence and death may seem a depressing subject, but its purpose is to make us appreciate each moment of our life. It encourages us to give up our obsession with the illusory appearances of this life so that we can work to create the causes for better rebirths, liberation, and enlightenment. Awareness of impermanence and death is a powerful way to cut through all our disturbing thoughts, such as anger. It also helps us to begin to understand the heart of the Buddha's teaching that oneself and all phenomena actually exist in a way that is completely free of the solid, fixed, and isolated way they now appear to us. If the thought of impermanence and death make you fearful or depressed, it is good to contemplate the benefits of having such awareness. This will provide some inspiration for doing the practice.

✦ PRELIMINARIES ✦

It is only as a fully enlightened being that I will be able to repay the kindness I have received from all sentient beings life after life.

Because of not realizing that everything is constantly changing and decaying, I completely waste my life in meaningless things, and I never have time to discover the true nature of my mind. I am not even able to create genuine happiness for myself, let alone for others. I must overcome all my attachments and afflicted thoughts to achieve enlightenment. The best way to do this is to realize the impermanence of all things and especially that I am going to die and can die at any time.

✦ THE MEDITATION ✦

Whatever I experience, as I experience it, appears to be permanent, unchanging. If it's attractive I think it will always be like that. If it brings up my aversion, it feels unbearable because it seems like this unpleasantness will go on forever.

If I use my wisdom and analyze my experiences, I can see that nothing in this world lasts.

But in my daily life I don't analyze; I just ignorantly grasp at appearances as being exactly as they appear. So attachment, anger, and every other suffering thought arise and disturb my mind.

Everything that appears to my mind only comes into existence by depending on causes and conditions. It's obvious that everything made by human beings depends on causes and conditions, but everything else does too.

My body itself came into existence depending on the substances of others, and it continues to depend on food, air, protection, and so forth.

The weather, vegetation, rivers, and mountains all arise depending on causes and conditions. The earth itself has come into existence depending on causes and conditions, as has the whole universe.

The Buddha taught that anything that exists depending on causes and conditions is impermanent—not simply changing moment by moment, but also decaying moment by moment.

I can see gross changes taking place as the weather changes, fashions come and go, ancient buildings fall into ruin, flowers die, friends grow old. But I never think—why?

These changes don't happen suddenly, but moment by moment. Because subtle change and decay occur moment by moment, sooner or later obvious change, aging, destruction, or death can be seen. A freshly cut flower is dead in a week. The decay takes place moment by moment.

How long is a moment? I can divide seconds into many milliseconds. Everything is changing, decaying even faster.

The Buddha said that impermanence exists simply because things come into existence depending on causes and conditions.

The sound of a bell ringing comes into existence depending on the bell, the clapper, the movement of an arm, and so forth. After a short time the sound dies away. Nothing stops it. It is unable to sustain itself. The sound depends on other things for its existence. When all the causes and conditions come together, a sound arises. But in the very next moment that original sound has decayed and in the next moment it decays further, and in the next, until no sound exists. It goes out of existence simply because it came into existence depending on causes and conditions.

Everything I experience, which appears to my mind to be so solid and static, is, in fact, constantly decaying. It is no more substantial or enduring than the sound of a bell.

This process of moment-by-moment decay is irreversible. Nothing can stop it.

Because there is birth, death has to come. It is inevitable.

This body of mine was born out of causes and conditions. Therefore it is impermanent; it is decaying and aging irreversibly all the time.

I will definitely die.

No matter how many friends or possessions I have, they cannot stop the process of decay. No matter how much wealth, power, influence, or knowledge I have, nothing can stop the process of aging. I am definitely going to die.

In my life I find so little time for practicing Dharma, the cause of real happiness. I must use my precious time, what little is left, to train my mind in the path to enlightenment.

Although my life is decaying moment by moment, I don't know when the very last moment will be. My lifespan isn't fixed.

People die at any age; even in the womb. Right now my existence and the world around me seem so solid. I can't imagine it could stop now. But thousands, perhaps millions of people have died at exactly my age.

Some people who were born after me have already died.

There are so many ways to die, so many things that could cause my death. There are so many diseases from which to die. People die from all sorts of accidents. Any one of these could happen to me. I can't imagine dying in a war or being murdered—but neither could all the people who died that way. Even the great bodhisattva Nagarjuna said it is a miracle to wake up each day!

There is really nothing that I can totally depend on to keep me alive. This is especially true these days when even the food, air, and water can be polluted or poisoned.

Is there anything I can think of that I could get or do that can definitely keep me alive?

This body is so fragile and so complex. Anything can go wrong at any time.

So I could die any time. Even now.

I should stop putting off practicing the Dharma. I must practice now!

Of all the things I depend on—family, friends, possessions, wealth— are any of them going to help me have a good death and a good rebirth? Won't my attachment to all these things be a great obstacle when I am trying to die peacefully? Won't there be a lot of fear to be suddenly and totally separated from all the things I have depended on?

If I practice well and try to develop genuine Dharma qualities such as refuge, love, or compassion, won't that be the best protection when I die?

So I'd better practice the Dharma, right now, and practice it purely.

✦ DEDICATION ✦

A Meditation on Refuge in the Three Jewels

Losang Dekyong (Angeles de la Torre)

✦ INTRODUCTION ✦

Since childhood we have been taking refuge in one thing or another to escape suffering and find happiness. First it was our parents, later it became our friends, lovers, money, and so on. Now we have the wisdom to see that a temporary and partial refuge is useless; we need a lasting, reliable, and complete solution to the ever-present problems of dissatisfaction and lack of happiness. What drives us to seek a genuine refuge is recognizing our valid fear of future suffering. What acts as the basis for choosing a refuge is trusting that it is complete, perfect, and reliable. This will give rise to admiration, devotion, and full confidence. Such faith is very important for our lives; it renews our life and gives us inner energy. It brings to us a new and fundamental attitude of not wanting to cause any harm to any being for any reason. The basic reason to take refuge is to free ourselves from suffering, but we can also take refuge because we cannot bear to see others suffer. Refuge is the door to liberation and enlightenment.

✦ PRELIMINARIES ✦

From this moment on, until I achieve enlightenment, I will meditate on refuge to gain the realization of complete faith in the Three Jewels, so that I may be able to become a refuge myself, with the power to help all sentient beings liberate themselves from suffering.

✦ THE MEDITATION ✦

At the present I have the good fortune of this human rebirth, which offers me the incredible opportunity of enlightenment in a short time. But even this fortunate human form is impermanent. Death will come sooner or later. At that time nothing can stop the ripening of the karma that will throw me into a new life. What sort of karma will that be?

Only actions motivated by pure love and compassion can help me. Am I confident I have done many truly virtuous actions in this life?

How often is my mind controlled by attachment, anger, jealousy, pride, and so on?

How many negative thoughts come to my mind during one day, even in one hour?

How much negative karma have I accumulated throughout this life? What about in past lives?

Even if my good karma does ripen, no matter what good rebirth I take, it will still be within cyclic existence and will be suffering and impermanent.

How can I leave myself so vulnerable, insecure, and uncertain knowing the potential suffering I face in future lives?

Why deceive myself by following the desires of my deluded mind which, at most, bring only temporary pleasure?

How can I rely merely on myself or on anyone or anything that is limited—whose compassion is limited, whose wisdom is undeveloped, and who is powerless to complete the task of achieving freedom from suffering?

Isn't it logical to depend on a perfect guide with a genuine method to show me the unmistaken path to liberation from cyclic existence?

So why are Buddha, Dharma, and Sangha worthy of all my confidence?

Since the Sangha evolves from the Dharma, and the Dharma comes from the Buddha, it follows that if the Buddha is a perfect refuge, then all the Three Jewels are a perfect refuge.

Why is the Buddha a perfect refuge? He has eliminated all faults and has developed the full potential of his mind and thereby possesses all good qualities.

Is this possible?

I can decide this by looking at my own mind: Do I recognize the potential of my own mind to change?

Do my delusions exist independently?

Are they an integral, fixed aspect of my mind?

Haven't I experienced the tendency of my mind to spontaneously give rise to peaceful, virtuous states, where distractions and confusion are diminished?

Can't I see people who are more wise and compassionate than I am?

If so, don't these things indicate the mind's perfectibility?

The Buddha has achieved that perfect mind. The Buddha has overcome all fears. The Buddha is the one being who is totally open, totally evolved. The Buddha's mind is limitless—it has limitless compassion, limitless wisdom, limitless power. It understands and sees conventional reality and ultimate truth simultaneously.

The Buddha has impartial love for all beings without exception. He does not distinguish beings as friend, enemy, or stranger.

The Buddha is skillful in showing us the path; he has developed comprehensive methods for others to achieve what he achieved.

All these things follow logically if there is perfect mind. It further follows that perfect mind manifests with a perfect body, perfect speech, and perfect skillful means. All of these help me and all beings remove the obscurations from our mind that cause suffering; they free our Buddha potential, which gives rise to every form of happiness and benefit.

Why can I take refuge in Dharma? Since the Dharma teachings come from the perfect mind of Buddha, they reveal the method I can follow to achieve that same state. It is a method that shows not only how to be free from wrong actions, but also how to be free from an uncontrolled mind and go beyond all confusion. It possesses the clarity, wisdom, and compassion of the Buddha, and it enables me to develop these qualities—the inherent potential of my mind. Since it comes from a mind totally free of harmful thoughts, it cannot harm me or others.

The Dharma is a refuge because it leads me to a deeper knowledge and experience of my inner nature, of my abilities, of my highest potential. Practicing Dharma is understanding more and more of my mind each day. This is the path the Buddha is showing me through refuge in the Jewel of Dharma.

Is faith in the Dharma enough to liberate me?

The Dharma shows me how I create a wrong view of myself that leads to wrong actions. I know I cannot continue to live like this anymore, complicating everything again and again, life after life, mortgaging my future lives. The Dharma reveals my present limitations, while showing that there exists in me and all beings the potential to be free of all suffering and experience pure wisdom and compassion. It is not enough to know this possibility exists; I have to connect with the Dharma methods that liberate my potential. Without the Dharma I haven't enough wisdom energy to liberate myself.

Why can I take refuge in the Sangha?

The supreme and magnificent community consists of those extraordinary beings who have achieved realization of the true nature of existence. They abide in wisdom. Therefore, they are completely qualified to help me improve my inner understanding. They are a source of inspiration, an aid on the path by showing that I too can practice and succeed just as they have. I can rely on them because they have impartial love for all beings.

✦ CONCLUSION ✦

From now until enlightenment, I will place my trust only in the perfect refuge of the Buddha, Dharma, and Sangha.

✦ DEDICATION ✦

A Meditation on Overcoming Attachment

Thubten Pemo (Linda Grossman)

✦ INTRODUCTION ✦

A variation of this meditation is to do it with an emphasis on the emptiness of the inquirer. As the mind engages in each inquiry, think that "I" and "my" are only products of self-grasping and attachment. Thus each question, for instance, "How am 'I' deceived?" becomes an even deeper inquiry.

✦ PRELIMINARIES ✦

✦ THE MEDITATION ✦

How am I deceived by attachment? It appears to bring happiness. I want something, and I do actions to get it. If I succeed, a temporary pleasant feeling arises, and I think I am happy. Then my mind thinks up another thing to get to make me feel good. Soon I run around doing things and saying things to get this other thing that I want. I feel unhappy when I don't get it. I feel good when I do get it. It never stops. I think of another thing to get, to make me feel happy. How many times do I do this in a day? In a week, a month, a year?

Craving-attachment keeps me busy and gives me a lot of work to do. Do I notice it is exhausting? Do I recognize I am exhausted by running after things to make me feel good? Or do I think life is okay and I am fine?

How much of what I get is real happiness? Was my vacation really as fantastic as I remember—or was it filled with both ups and downs? As I notice this, I am drawn to my other memories of happiness. How much of my memory is selective and has come to suit my craving?

If I really look, I seem to think that craving causes happiness. Yet when craving arises, I can see my mind is not peaceful. In fact, I'm often confused about what I'm craving. I want a vacation, but I also want financial security. I am conflicted about what to chase. Is a two-week vacation worth five thousand dollars? But again I am deceived, thinking this is the choice. I know worldly pleasures cannot bring, or cause, happiness. But I forget this fact and trust in worldly pleasures, sense pleasures, pleasures that arise due to people, places, and things. How often do I do this? How often do I behave as if craving is the only choice?

As I look deeply, I can see that craving-attachment causes suffering. Even in this life, I've suffered numberless times because of attachment. I've cried so many tears and broken my heart so many times. But then I forget and do it again. How do I begin to get some control over my attachment?

I must understand deeply, at the most visceral level, that happiness is possible and that following my attachment causes unhappiness. Attachment causes even more unhappiness than it gives temporal happiness. It is a cause of unhappiness in the same way that cherishing myself is a cause of unhappiness; attachment is just another form of self-cherishing—the cause of my suffering. I am deceived by my own beliefs, so I experience countless sufferings in all my lives.

I must also understand deeply that my mind is obscured. I have just seen that what is "unhappiness" I've mistakenly labeled as "happiness." I made it up because I thought feeling good, even for a moment, was happiness. I believed what my mind made up. My delusions actually cause suffering and unhappiness, not happiness. If I can understand what I truly want, then I can decide to really abandon my delusions.

I know I want happiness, but do I really understand what that is? Do I really believe in what I need to do to get it? Do my actions reflect this? What do I do to hurt myself? What have I done to give happiness to myself?

If I want happiness, I simply need to stop causing myself suffering and cultivate happiness. How? It is a process of developing awareness, cultivating determination, and actually doing. But it is a long and difficult process. Sometimes I am so confused and do not understand these basic, simple facts. Instead, I follow delusions when they arise, give power to them, and expect to have happiness as the result. I continue to do non-virtuous actions and don't know why I am unhappy.

But if I really understand my goals and how I am deceived, I will make progress. As I do, I can acknowledge my progress, however small, and rejoice in it. I can rejoice simply because I am working to give up craving-attachment. After a lot of work, there is a little bit of progress. That small progress is a true cause of happiness in my mind, and I become encouraged to continue the work of giving up craving-attachment. Thus I experience greater and greater joy, happiness, and inner peace.

As I do my analysis though, I must be wary of straying; I must stay on track, be clear, and be aware of what I am abandoning. So what do I give up? I am not giving up sense objects or pleasant feelings—only the attachment that craves happiness. It is not an attitude of rejecting the world but rather of being objective about my experiences of pleasure and pain. Feelings come and go, and it is possible to experience them without craving. I can do that. Why? Because ignorance is the cause of attachment. Ultimately I am working to abandon ignorance and realize the empty nature of myself and of all phenomena. Who is there to crave? What is there to crave after? The problem is not within the object of my attachment; the problem comes from my own mind. So my way of thinking and perceiving must change. Then I will see things as they really are, and I will have succeeded in my goal.

✦ DEDICATION ✦

A Meditation on the Factors Stimulating the Arising of Disturbing Attitudes and Emotions

Thubten Chodron (Cherry Green)

✦ INTRODUCTION ✦

This meditation is best done after reflecting on the four noble truths and the six root disturbing attitudes and emotions.

The key to getting some taste when we meditate on Lamrim is to relate the points to our own lives. In this case, by reflecting on each point one by one and finding examples of it in our lives, we will come to understand how the following six factors affect the arisal of negative emotions and misconceptions in our minds.

✦ PRELIMINARIES ✦

Begin your meditation as usual with the preliminary prayers, generating a bodhichitta motivation and doing a few minutes of breathing meditation to calm the mind.

✦ THE MEDITATION ✦

The predispositions of the disturbing attitudes and emotions
Until I realize emptiness directly, the predispositions of disturbing

attitudes and emotions remain in my mindstream. For example, I may not be angry at this moment, but the seed of anger is in my mindstream. When it meets the proper conditions (some of which are below), that seed transforms into full-blown anger.

Reflect: these seeds are ever present in my mind and can ripen at any moment in my life to create the cause of suffering.

Contact with the object
(this includes people, places, ideas, etc.)

When I meet an object I find pleasant, attachment arises. When I meet an object I find unpleasant, aversion arises.

What are the main objects of attachment for me?

What are the main objects of anger for me?

Until I gain more control of my mind I should follow the Buddha's recommendation to temporarily avoid contact with objects and people that trigger the strongest attachments and aversions.

What objects do I need to keep a respectful distance from?

How can I relate in a more balanced way to the objects and people I encounter?

Detrimental influences such as wrong friends

Reflect on the following points:

How much of my life is influenced by peer pressure?

How easily do I adopt the values and actions of my friends and family?

What qualities do I look for in people? Who do I choose as friends?

Are they people with good ethical discipline and a kind heart, or do they speak badly behind others' backs or lie when it suits their own purposes?

Do they encourage me in my interest in, or practice of, the Dharma, or make fun of it?

Out of friendship for them, do I get discouraged or distracted from going to Dharma classes, attending retreats, or doing practice at home?

Am I able to do what I know to be right even if a friend or family member does not agree and pressures me to change?

Verbal stimulus and media: (books, television, magazines, news-papers, radio, Internet, CDs, etc.)

Check: How much of the past week was spent being exposed to the media—listening to the radio in the car, channel surfing on the TV, exploring the Internet?

If I am honest with myself, how much is done for a good reason, and how much is distraction?

How much do I fill my eyes, ears, and mind with media stimuli to avoid looking at what is really going on inside of myself?

How much does the media shape my self-image and what I believe?

Make a determination concerning your relationship to the media.

Habits

What emotional habits or patterns do I have?

Observe the emotions that commonly distract you when you meditate. Observe your habitual behavior—emotional, verbal, and physical. For example:

Am I usually grumpy in the morning?

Am I sensitive about my weight, looks, or athletic abilities?

Am I easily offended by the comments of others?

Am I continuously searching for romantic relationships?

What are my emotional "buttons"?

Do I know the antidotes to these patterns and habits?

Make a determination to learn and apply the antidotes.

Inappropriate attention

Do I pay attention to the negative aspects of situations?

Do I have numerous biases?

Am I quick to jump to conclusions or be judgmental?

How much do I look at situations only in terms of how they affect me and those I'm attached to?

How much am I able to see the bigger picture, including others' needs and concerns?

What steps can I take to remedy these tendencies?

✦ CONCLUSION ✦

Having understood the disadvantages of the disturbing attitudes, I must work to abandon them. I must make an effort to learn how to avoid or subdue the factors causing their arisal. Doing this will bring peace in this life, enable me to abandon negative karma, and create positive potential. It will also bring me closer to enlightenment and will actively contribute to world peace.

✦ DEDICATION ✦

A Meditation on Karma

Losang Drimay (Karen Gudmundsson)

✦ INTRODUCTION ✦

Karma, a Sanskrit word meaning action, refers to the process of mental imprints turning into the experiences of our life. These imprints are formed through everything we consciously do, say, or think. In fact, it is the thoughts that are most crucial because they are the source of our verbal and physical actions.

Karma is a difficult subject to understand through either observation or reasoning. We might be able to deduce a general theory about karma just by pondering, but only a buddha, a fully awakened being, can directly see the specific workings of karma. So we must rely on valid authority for most of what we know about karma. Fortunately, the Buddhist scriptures go into extensive detail on this subject, Shakyamuni Buddha giving us examples from his own past lives as well as lists of certain actions to avoid and others to practice in order to get out of our suffering.

The following meditation is one I developed during a long retreat on the Graduated Path (Lamrim). The content is drawn strictly from scripture while the format is based only loosely on traditional methods.

I use the imagery of a garden to represent the important points of this topic so as to make the contemplation more engaging. The Buddhist teachings are rich with symbolism and metaphors, especially agricultural ones; but remember these are only symbols, not the actual thing. Karma is like a seed, but is not actually a seed. In the karma garden, I use both traditional imagery and my own.

The karma garden is just one section of my Lamrim Park. Other sections include a perfect human rebirth daycare center and a samsara playground. You can create your own park.

✦ PRELIMINARIES ✦

Rest your awareness on the sensation of your breath as you inhale and exhale. Do this for at least ten breaths in order to still the mind.

✦ MEDITATION ✦

Now visualize yourself walking through the Lamrim Park along the steppingstones that lead to your karma garden. Open the gate, pass through, and look around.

At the far end is an orchard with various fruit trees. A fruit tree is not something that appears or disappears quickly, but rather tends to stay put relative to the rest of the garden. The fruit trees represent your throwing karma: the karma that determines what sort of life form you have: human, animal, spirit, and so forth. At the end of your previous lifetime a very strong mental imprint came to the forefront of your mind, encouraged by whatever mental state was predominant at that time, and propelled you into this life. Like the fruit trees, it is a long-term, fixed result.

How does being a human shape the way I experience this life? How would my life be different if I were not a human?

Around the edges of the garden are banks of flowers and ornamental plants. These represent the background of your life, your environmental karma. Even the things in your world that seem unrelated to you personally, such as the weather and political events, still appear to you as results of your own past actions and the imprints those actions laid down on your mind. Everything you perceive comes by way of your own mental conditioning; they appear to you in a certain way because you have the propensity to see things that way.

What kind of environment do I live in?

Now turn your attention to the vegetable garden. There are some crops, such as corn and beans, that yield a harvest that is the same as the seed you planted. You plant a bean, which is the very seed of a bean plant, and you harvest bean seeds to eat. This represents the karma of habits. You have a tendency toward certain types of thoughts, words, and physical actions because you have done the same type of thing before, not only in this life but in previous lives. You have done it before, so you do it again, and the cycle continues. Children come into this life with distinctive temperaments, some enjoying killing animals, for example, and others being horrified by killing. This comes from their past-life habit of either killing or not killing.

What kind of habits and mental tendencies do I have?

There are other rows of vegetables, such as lettuce and carrots, where the seed is not the harvested part, yet the seed that was planted caused the harvested part. The lettuce and carrots represent the type of karma that ripens as things that happen to you directly. If you did something to harm someone in a past life, that harm comes back to you. If it is happening to you now, that means you did it to someone else before, for better or worse. If you are prosperous now, you must have been generous and supported others in the past. If someone harms you now, you must have harmed them in the past. Like the leaves of the lettuce, which correspond to the seed that was planted, you also get a result that corresponds to the seeds you plant.

What kind of experiences do I tend to have? What can these experiences show me about my actions in the past?

You have learned so much on this first visit. Sit down on a swinging bench to let it all sink in: The orchard, which is the karma that propelled you into this life; the ornamental plants, forming the background of your life; the seed crops, which are your karmic habits; and the other vegetable crops, which correspond precisely with what you planted in the past.

Make a plan to study more about how karma works so that you can come back later and add more detail to this garden.

Now get up and walk out the garden gate. Coming to the park entrance, this session is finished.

❖   DEDICATION   ❖

A Meditation on Equanimity

Thubten Losang (Tony Wengoborsky)

✦ PRELIMINARIES ✦

Begin with the motivation of attaining buddhahood for the benefit of all sentient beings. Focus for a moment and really think about what this means.

✦ THE MEDITATION ✦

Now imagine that well hidden in a forest is a small clearing. In the middle, below a grass-covered mound of earth, is a foxhole, the home of a beautiful young female fox and her four babies. It is early spring, but still frosty, and the surface of a small brook that runs just in front of the foxhole is still partially frozen. Inside, the four little foxes are constantly hungry, and so the new mother is very busy, moving frequently in and out of the den to feed her little ones.

Pause a moment and try to visualize this vividly.

One day the mother fox steps out into the pitch-black darkness of the early morning, carefully takes scent, then starts to slowly trot along her habitual path close to the brook. After only a few steps, she walks into the heavy metal trap that was set there, skillfully hidden under dry leaves and tiny twigs. The sudden violence of the trap's huge jaws closing around her right hind leg throws the animal to the ground, and a terrible wave of excruciating pain penetrates the fox's crooked body.

Writhing in mad confusion, she forcefully tries to pull her leg out of the trap, but with every movement of her body the well-sharpened teeth of the trap penetrate deeper into her torn flesh, and she cannot escape. She tries again and again, helplessly twisting her body in all directions, but to no avail.

She pauses, but the power of her instinct of survival and of motherly responsibility urges the mother fox to quickly continue her hopeless struggle. This instinct now tells her to sacrifice her leg in order to free herself, so she starts gnawing on her hind leg. She sinks her teeth into her own flesh, tearing away at it, biting, gnawing, ripping her skin off, and whimpering from time to time in her agonizing pain. But the trap's jaws snared her thigh too close to the body, and her violent biting causes her to bleed more and more, and with another instinct, the mother fox abandons her desperate attempt to sever the leg from her body. And for the first time since she has been caught in the trap, the excruciating pain, maddening terror, rage, and despair overwhelm our fox mother, and the hoarse wailing of the tormented animal pierces the cold silence of the forest.

At this point, pause and imagine this vividly.

Some ten to fifteen miles away, a trapper sits in front of his cabin, cleaning his rifle. The day before, while carrying firewood, he slipped on a wet branch and seriously hurt his foot. Being hardly able to walk, he decided to forego for today the daily round of checking his traps. The trapper knows well that fur trapping is prohibited during the period of reproduction, but having spent almost two full winter months sick and bedridden, he now considers the trapping essential to ensure his own material well-being, and indeed, his own survival.

Pause again and imagine this vividly.

The dim light of the next day's cold morning finds our mother fox dead. Her distorted body is covered with blood, mud, and urine; her tarnished eyes, wide open in terror, face the leaden sky. They are the eyes of a young female fox that died of loss of blood, exhaustion, and cold— and of the broken heart of a mother who knows her children will die.

At this point, pause for a while and really observe the meditation's effect on your mind.

When you are ready, continue to meditate, taking time to analyze the following points:

Contemplate: it is most probable that I carry in my mindstream numberless karmic potentials apt to project me into a life similar to that of the mother fox, her babies, or the trapper—at any moment, even today!

Consider the nature of karma, the importance of purification, and the opportunities of one's own precious life.

Try to recall and vividly imagine the intense physical and mental suffering of the mother fox for a little while. Then ask yourself: could I bear this?

Closely examine the way in which the mother fox and the trapper appear to exist in the perceiving mind. Notice feelings, judgments, and certainties.

Would my view of victim and evildoer change if I imagined the fox killing a litter of helpless newborn rabbits?

What happens if I visualize the trapper risking his life to journey several days in the dead of winter in order to assure a veterinarian's treatment for one of his huskies that has been severely injured?

I should examine the true nature of my perceptions and how things are.

Contemplate: If I feel compassion for the fox and her babies, but aversion or hatred toward the trapper, then I haven't even started to understand Buddha Shakyamuni's message of universal responsibility toward all beings. I can cut myself off completely from another by my judgment. Without impartiality, great compassion cannot arise.

Consider the possibility of feeling equal love and compassion for both the foxes and the trapper.

Then consider: In fact the objects worthy of the most intense compassion and care are definitely those sentient beings who cause great harm to others, because they are in danger of incurring the greatest, most terrible sufferings. What is my habitual response to those who cause great harm to others?

✦ DEDICATION ✦

Conclude your meditation by directing any beneficial energy generated in your mindstream through your efforts of directly working on your mind toward the rapid, complete, and unobstructed attainment of the realizations aimed at in the motivation that you formulated in the beginning of the session. Ideally this should be the motivation to attain buddhahood for the benefit of all foxes, all trappers, and all other suffering sentient beings.

A Meditation on the Kindness of Sentient Beings

Tenzin Dasel (Siliana Bosa)

Take time to feel comfortable. Relax and release the tension from your body. Let go of all thoughts and be aware of your posture starting from the head. Let go of tension in the muscles of your face. Go slowly down the body, feeling the release of tension from all the muscles of your neck, shoulders, and arms, right down to your feet. Gradually you feel pervaded by a natural calmness.

Be aware of the space of your body. Be aware of the feeling of your body on the cushion.

✦ THE MEDITATION ✦

Part A (or you can go directly to Part B)
Analyze the feeling of stability of the earth element of your body. The characteristic of the earth element is to be obstructive. It consists of all the solid parts of the body, such as the bones, flesh, and so on.

Then gradually bring your attention to the water element within your body. The characteristic of the water element is to be wet and fluid. It consists of all the liquids of the body: blood, saliva, urine, and so forth.

Then gradually bring your attention to the fire element within your body. The characteristic of the fire element is to burn and to help digestion. Feel the warmth that spreads all over your body.

Part B

Slowly bring your attention to the air that is touching your body, touching your face, and through the nostrils, entering the body. The characteristic of the air element is mobility. It is what allows all movement of the body, and what supports our life from the moment of our birth to the moment of our death; it is always with us until our end.

Be aware of the sensation you have at the nostrils while watching the in-going and out-going of your breath. You can count "one" for each full cycle of in and out. Try to count up to ten.

As soon you note any thought arising in your mind, bring your attention back to the breath, only to the breath, and start to count again from "one." Bring your attention back to the breath again and again. Start to count again from "one," over and over again. Contemplate for between three to seven minutes.

Then contemplate as follows: The fact that I can contemplate my breath is because I am human, endowed with the special intelligence of a human being. One of the abilities of the mind is to be able to concentrate on whatever object I want. I can only be aware of the breath because I am still alive, and that depends upon many different causes and conditions, such as the balance of the elements within the body. That I am still alive is thanks to my parents, particularly thanks to the kindness of my mother. She has looked after me from the time when I was just born, completely helpless. If there had not been people cleaning me, dressing me, giving me food, and so on, I wouldn't be alive now.

Contemplate: From the time of my birth up to now, how many beings have supported my life? There were those who gave me an education and advice. Everything I have, all the comforts I enjoy—the house where I live, the clothes I am wearing, the food I eat—all of these come from others, from their efforts, energy, and even from their lives.

Try to make this thought as vast as possible, by finding and adding your own personal examples.

Then think: My life it is totally dependent on others. Even this body comes from the positive energy that I accumulated in all my past lives through the practice of morality based on not harming and on helping others. So all living beings are the cause of my happiness.

Definitely what I receive from others is much more than what I give. Without others I can't have even a glass of water. I'm not at all self-sufficient.

Generate a sense of appreciation for what you receive from others.

Again think: All these living beings are exactly like myself in wanting to be happy and free from problems. We all have the right to pursue this by appropriate means.

All living beings are exactly like myself in trying to find peace and happiness. Each is making efforts according to his or her own capacities, intelligence, and potential. They all try to get rid of problems and achieve at least a temporary release from their tensions and sufferings.

We are all the same; there is no difference at all.

Contemplate this in as vast a way as possible. Make your mind one with this understanding of interdependence and equanimity. Extend a sense of caring toward others up to the generation of a spontaneous feeling of love and compassion, recognizing that all living beings, in order to grow, need affection, and this is also what makes us all the same.

Contemplate: We all have an innate fundamental nature of kindness. I have already the potential to protect others from unpleasant experiences by not killing, not stealing, not using harsh words, and so on. So, since we are all the same and everything that I have comes from others, it is wise and logical to stop harming others, and to be aware of all the actions of my body, speech, and mind.

Not harming others, developing a good heart, and protecting the mind from disturbing thoughts are the teachings of the Buddha. Buddha Shakyamuni is the embodiment of all these qualities. It was by relying on this human potential that he achieved limitless qualities.

Contemplate: These same qualities are latent in my mental continuum. The Buddha represents the qualities I can achieve.

Visualize the Buddha, in the nature of transparent light, in front of yourself. From the heart of the Buddha, light emanates in all the ten directions, touching your heart and the hearts of all living beings. In that moment, by feeling the contact with this light, imagine that your mind and the minds of all beings are purified or liberated from the confusion that prevents us from experiencing the limitless potential of our mind.

Contemplate like that with a strong sense of refuge in the Three Jewels and in the buddha potential of yourself and all beings.

✦ DEDICATION ✦

May all the positive energy that I have developed in this meditation result in all my actions of body, speech, and mind becoming expressions of love, compassion, and wisdom.

May all the beings who see me, remember me, or come into contact with me be immediately released from suffering. May they experience only great joy and happiness so that they generate positive thoughts that will bring about their future everlasting happiness.

May I be a wish-fulfilling friend for all beings and bring them good fortune.

Remember this throughout the day and never forget that the purpose of life is to be happy in order to bring happiness to all mother sentient beings.

A Meditation on Exchanging
Self with Others

Tenzin Dekyi (Chantal Carrerot)

✦ PRELIMINARIES ✦

Prepare for the day by generating a special motivation through the distinctive positive thought: Today, I am dedicating all my activities to the welfare of living beings. Let the altruistic state of mind wishing to benefit others be the driving force and inspiration for all my actions today.

✦ THE MEDITATION ✦

There is no difference between others and myself. Twenty-four hours a day I am trying to obtain something good for myself and to avoid any unpleasantness, problems, or suffering. Others are also striving to secure happiness and avoid suffering. Whatever they are doing, whatever their appearance, whatever way they dress, whatever manners they display, or whatever opinions they may hold, they are just trying to be happy. Just like I am.

Their happiness is no less important to them than my happiness is to me. Nor does the suffering they experience hurt them less than the pain I myself encounter. In that respect, we are completely equal. Nobody has any more right to happiness than anybody else.

However there is a difference: others are innumerable and I am only one person. Just like one dollar is nothing compared to one million dollars, wouldn't it be fair to consider one person's happiness insignificant compared to infinite others' happiness?

In terms of results, there is a significant difference between the self-centered attitude that considers self-happiness a priority and the attitude that cherishes others first. Self-centeredness is the source of all misery. Cherishing others is the source of all happiness. Therefore it is appropriate to dedicate myself to work for the benefit of others. To use others simply for my own welfare is totally wrong.

In order to shift the focus of concern from self to others, I will infuse my mind with an understanding of the disadvantages of the egoistic attitude and the value of the attitude that cherishes others.

Contemplate the following drawbacks and advantages by relating them to actual situations in your own life:

The wish to secure my happiness first creates a very narrow perspective. From that selfish attitude, many fears come that make me nervous and uptight. When things do not work out the way I want them to, they appear worse than they really are. At the end, I feel overwhelmed by the misery I have myself created, and I become unable to bear the slightest harm or tolerate any hardship.

I approach situations with the thought, "What is there for me to gain?" Being so worried about getting something for myself, there is no opportunity to relax. Instead many opportunities for getting upset arise.

Likewise, in my relations to others, I expect that they will like me, treat me well, help me, and respect me. Therefore I am disappointed when they behave otherwise. I become overly sensitive and easily hurt; the slightest unpleasant word or criticism becomes unbearable, and I always feel uncomfortable.

Because I value my welfare most, I am at risk of conflicts with others. My exaggerated self-concern creates a barrier between myself and others and alienates me from them. Being insensitive to their needs, I act against their wishes. How could any harmony derive from such an attitude?

Because I reject them, they appear negative to me and I see many faults with them. If, on the contrary, I start caring for them, they will appear in a more positive light, and that will bring some happiness to both of us.

This self-centered attitude is the source of most delusions. Because of it, I become envious of others. Instead of rejoicing at their good fortune and partaking in it, I belittle them and have no tolerance for their mistakes. Due to attachment to myself, I overlook the impact of my actions on them and fail to practice the basic training of ethics. Various negative emotions cloud my mind, creating numerous distractions and obscurations, and I cannot develop any concentration. Because of the obscurations in my mind, I am also unable to develop any wisdom. Therefore the whole path to liberation is blocked.

This egotism prevents me from respecting others, particularly spiritual teachers, and learning from them. It stops me from developing love and compassion. It tightens my heart and brings spiritual suffocation. It is a huge obstacle to reaching peace and happiness.

The attitude of being more concerned with the happiness of others reverses the egoistic attitude of clinging to one's happiness and all of its shortcomings. The negative types of mind—attachment, dissatisfaction, anger—become less powerful the more I cherish others.

Not only does cherishing others make them feel good, it also makes me feel good. It makes me feel good about others and about myself. It remedies feelings of guilt and self-loathing. In fact, the more I care for others, the more I feel satisfied.

By caring about others, the focus is taken away from me, and my mind widens its perspective. My problems appear less important and don't bother me so much. When I cherish others, I feel close to them; communication becomes easier and they also feel drawn to me.

Through voluntarily taking the responsibility to solve the problems of others and benefit them, I develop courage and inner strength. All spiritual qualities follow from such an attitude.

How wonderful it would be if all sentient beings had happiness!

How wonderful if they were completely free from all the problems, worries, pains, sicknesses, sufferings of birth, old age, and death!

How wonderful if they were to abide in a state of stable peace and satisfaction that never changes into suffering! May they abide in such a state!

✦ CONCLUSION ✦

Today in all my activities, I will practice seeing others as important and cherishing them. In every interaction I have with them, I will focus on their well-being rather than on getting something for myself.

The purpose of my life and of today is to benefit others as much as possible. Dedicating myself to others is what makes my day and every day worthwhile.

✦ DEDICATION ✦

A Meditation on Loving-Kindness

Thubten Gyatso (Adrian Feldman)

✦ PRELIMINARIES ✦

Sit in a comfortable position with your back straight. Generate the motivation to meditate in order to repay the kindness of all beings. Then focus your whole attention upon the coming and going of your breath at your nostrils, breathing more deeply and more slowly than usual, for about eight minutes.

Now, let go of the breathing and focus your attention upon the clear and still nature of your mind. Your mind is awareness. By nature, it is capable of experiencing things as they are without distortion. Try to experience the clear nature of your mind, uninterrupted by the movement of thought patterns, for five minutes.

✦ THE MEDITATION ✦

Place your attention at your heart chakra—the midpoint inside the chest—the seat of your emotions. Do not think that you are looking down from your head; simply try to feel that the subjective mind itself is based at the heart.

Think of somebody close to you; imagine them blissfully happy, receiving all they want. Generate loving-kindness—pure, unconditional delight in their happiness—and observe that it has a physical sensation of warmth that arises at your heart, like fresh warm water flowing into

61

a cold bath. Imagine it continuously pouring out and growing stronger. The healing energy of loving-kindness spreads throughout your body and mind and takes on the appearance of brilliant, white nectar. This brings bliss wherever it touches and simultaneously heals all of your physical and mental problems and their causes. Your entire body is filled with the blissful, radiant, healing, white nectar of loving-kindness. Your bones, organs, muscles, and so on, dissolve into this nectar.

Concentrate upon this for a few minutes.

The nectar is extremely bright. Shining like a supernova, you send out countless rays of loving-kindness through the pores of your skin in all directions. These rays touch the hearts of all universal beings, cleanse them, and bring every happiness up to the bliss of enlightenment.

First, a beam of nectar goes to your mother who is sitting on your left, then to your father who is sitting on your right.

Then it goes to your remaining friends and relatives behind you and finally to all those who have made you angry or upset, recently or in the past, who are sitting in front of you.

Forgive the harm they have caused you and have compassion for the harm they are causing themselves. Then send the light to all other sentient beings—in human aspect—all around, as far as the horizon.

Think that you have brought all suffering throughout the universe to an end. The beings have become buddhas, and their environments have become pure lands. Rejoice that you have repaid the kindness of all beings, your mothers. Having completed its work, the blissful energy of loving-kindness flows back into you.

All that you have visualized dissolves into the blissful dharmakaya, and you remain like a bubble of light floating in empty space.

Now, like condensed breath upon a mirror slowly evaporating, your body gradually disappears from the outside in; the last part to go is at your heart. All that remains is your blissful mind, focused single-pointedly upon your ultimate nature—emptiness—which appears like the first hint of light in the dark sky before dawn. Hold this concentration for as long as you can.

Generate the blissful healing energy of loving-kindness once again. This appears as white light that takes the form of your body with your mind inside.

Feel that your old body and mind—products of karma and affliction—have gone forever, and your present body and mind are now produced from wisdom and compassion.

Think: The entire purpose of my existence is to bring happiness to others and to ease their burden of suffering however I can. From now on I will instantly dispel the slightest hint of self-importance from my mind, and I will always work for others with every action I do, every word I speak, and every thought I think.

✦ DEDICATION ✦

Strongly dedicate the positive energy of this meditation to that attainment.

A Meditation on Love and Compassion

Lobsang Tarchin (Lorenzo Rossello)

Over the years various organizations have been formed in the world for the promotion of peace, but that peace, which is much wished for, remains elusive. Why is this? Shakyamuni Buddha taught that peace cannot be achieved unless we directly act to create the causes that bring about peace. We need to look inside ourselves and not outside for the actual causes of peace. Externally we might be able to establish some favorable conditions for peace, but we remain unable to create its substantial cause since this is directly connected with our mind and its accompanying mental factors. Until we are able to completely eliminate the afflictive emotions—the negative mental states of ignorance, attachment, hatred, and so forth—and generate virtuous qualities such as love, compassion, patience, and wisdom, our heart-mind will never be able to abide in a state of lasting peace and happiness.

If a single individual abides with a pacified, serene state of mind, endowed with virtuous qualities, there can be more peace and harmony within a couple. If there is peace and serenity within a couple, there can also be peace and serenity within a family. If there is peace and serenity in a family, there can also be peace and serenity in a community, in groups, and in nations.

✦ PRELIMINARIES ✦

✦ THE MEDITATION ✦

I was born in dependence on my father and mother. Only due to their kindness was I able to survive and grow, since I was born completely helpless and unprotected. My education was the result of the kindness and patience of my teachers during my studies at school. My knowledge has also developed in dependence on relationships with my friends, because it was with them that I verified my beliefs and discussed my uncertainties.

Each moment of happiness, each positive experience requires an interpersonal relationship, whether between family members, friends, partners, or even between teachers and disciples.

Everything, every possession I enjoy is the result of some form of kindness received from other beings. The meat I eat and the milk I drink come from the kindness of cows. The leather shoes and the clothes I wear come from the kindness of the animals that gave their skins and their wool. The vegetables, cereals, and fruit I eat are due to the hard work of many farmers. Each type of machine or object I use is the result of many hours of hard work by workers, managers, and administrators of various industries. The house in which I live protects my body from the heat, cold, and harm of the elements; it too is the result of the work of builders, carpenters, engineers, architects, and others.

The environment in all its multifarious aspects—which I often consider to be only pleasant landscapes of lakes, mountains, woods, the sea—involves me and all beings in a relationship of interdependence since it is the basis of our very existence. Who doesn't want to live in a clean, harmonious, uncontaminated environment? Just by looking at it, my mind becomes calm and I feel relaxed.

By clearly recognizing the web of interdependent relationships that support me, surely I must conclude how important it is to cultivate non-violent actions toward all beings and toward the environment itself. This is possible only if I possess a love that wishes others true happiness, and a compassion that wishes all others be free of every kind of suffering.

By the power of compassion I will be able to avoid harming others. By the power of love I will try to benefit others. These should be supported by the wisdom realizing all phenomena are empty of true existence. I need to have compassion and to manifest it with wisdom and to benefit others by means of love based on wisdom.

Visualize in the space in front of you all these sentient beings who are pervaded by the various kinds of sufferings that come from being controlled by delusion and karma.

May all these beings, without exception, be completely free from suffering and its causes.

Try to generate your heart-mind into the very manifestation of compassion so it becomes one with compassion. One-pointedly concentrate upon this compassion; stabilize it and maintain it for as long as possible.

Then think: The greatest power human beings can generate is kindness. Through loving-kindness it is possible to pacify and subdue every mind.

Generate love to all sentient beings who lack happiness and its causes. By the force of this thought, ensure that your heart-mind is generated into love itself.

✦ CONCLUSION ✦

I will use each circumstance of my everyday life—work, study, travel, and even those things that are difficult—to put my experiences during meditation into practice. Only by doing this will I be able to destroy the actual enemy, the afflictive emotions, and to create the causes for true peace. All my actions performed for the benefit of others should be done in a kind and respectful way.

✦ DEDICATION ✦

A Meditation on Patience

Tenzin Dongak (Fedor Stracke)

Patience is having an undisturbed mind even while encountering problems or while being harmed by people. We need to be able to keep our peace of mind and not lose our love and compassion for others.

Once the conditions for harmful intent—the seed of habituation in the mind, closeness to the object, and wrong conceptualization—are complete, harmful intent will arise whether we want it or not. At present we are subconsciously conditioned to regard anger as something beneficial; therefore, we have a willingness to become angry. To overcome this conditioning we need to think very deeply about the faults of becoming angry and the benefits of practicing patience.

❖ PRELIMINARIES ❖

In the space in front of you, visualize Chenrezig, indivisible in nature from your root guru. Chenrezig embodies the compassion of all the buddhas and manifests as a youthful deity, white in color, and seated on a lotus. His body is adorned with fine jewels and garments. Between two hands he holds a jewel, and two other hands hold a rosary and lotus.

Then request twice from the depths of your heart: "Please bless my mindstream that I may be able to generate the perfection of patience and completely abandon anger."

67

With the first repetition visualize white light coming down from the guru-deity, purifying your mind-body continuum of all obscurations.

With the second repetition visualize all the realizations of the guru deity coming down in the form of orange light completely filling you up.

✦ THE MEDITATION ✦

Contemplate the benefits of patience:
If I have the cool stream of patience that pacifies the fires of anger, I won't suffer from losing my mental happiness. I will have fewer enemies and less interference in the future. I will experience happiness in this life, close the door to lower rebirths, and experience the happiness of higher rebirths and liberation. At the time of death I can die without regrets. If I am reborn as a human, I will have a beautiful form. The bodhisattva Shantideva said: "Whoever abandons anger will be happy in this and in future lives."

Contemplate the disadvantages of anger:
There is no negative emotion as destructive as anger. The Buddha taught that just one instant of anger has many negative results. Not only does anger create negative karma that will ripen as suffering, it also destroys positive states of mind already generated and prevents the generation and abiding of future ones.

Contemplate the following points to gain a clear understanding of this:
There are some aspects of anger I can see:
When my mind is poisoned by anger I cannot experience peace.
Existing joy and happiness are destroyed and are difficult to gain again.
Mental stability arising from equanimity is also destroyed.
It robs me of my sleep and harms my health.
As Asanga said in the *Uttaratantra,* "The arousal of anger gives pain in the heart."
Having a stressed and unhappy mind is one of the main conditions for anger to arise. Therefore, at all times, I should preserve my mental equanimity and happiness. Shantideva advised: "If I can do something

about my problem then there is no benefit to getting upset. If I can do nothing about my problem then there is also no point in getting upset."

Therefore, I also need to contemplate the main unseen aspects of anger:

It destroys the merits I have accumulated from doing virtuous actions over a thousand eons.

It delays my progress along the path for one eon.

Each moment of anger results in one eon in the hells.

When reborn human I will be ugly.

Every time I get angry it leaves a karmic potential on my mindstream, which reinforces and increases my mental pattern of anger, thereby ensuring that I have to experience all the suffering results again and again.

Contemplate the patience of not letting yourself be affected by harm:
Bodhisattvas who are harmed think, "This poor person is under the control of the demon of anger. So I shouldn't get angry but feel compassion because this person is suffering. I should help this person, not harm him."

Someone under the influence of anger is like a person under the influence of alcohol; she has no control over her actions. Once the conditions for harmful intent are complete, it will arise whether she wants it or not, and she is compelled to engage in a harmful action that inflicts suffering on others.

Recall a time when somebody said something disagreeable or insulting. Analyze if any harm was actually received.

What harmed me?

How was I harmed?

Aren't the insulting words merely sounds traveling from the mouth of the other person to my ear and then registered in my mind?

Has any harm really been received?

No, this harm is completely my own mental fabrication. It does not even exist conventionally. In fact, it is completely nonexistent, just like the horns of a rabbit!

Meditate on happiness by thinking:
How great! I have not been harmed! I still have buddha nature, the potential to achieve buddhahood and benefit countless sentient beings,

just like the Buddha. The intrinsic nature of my mind is still clear light, completely pure and unstained.

Since this being did not harm me, there is no basis for my anger; the only thing that can really harm me is my own anger.

My antagonists should actually be objects of my compassion since they are tormented by disturbing thoughts and emotions and they create negative karma in dependence on me. They are showing me the need to practice more, to act like a bodhisattva, and to become a buddha to truly help others.

Contemplate the following points to develop the patience of being able to bear difficulties:

If I see only the negative side of antagonists and problems, I will be overwhelmed. I must see the beneficial side of experiencing problems.

Problems and hardships are very kind to me. They can:

Teach me to avoid nonvirtue if I want to avoid the same suffering in the future.

Teach me to practice virtue if I want to experience happiness and a happy rebirth.

Cause me to generate renunciation and thereby lead me to liberation.

Teach me about the suffering of others and through this to generate compassion and bodhichitta and lead me to enlightenment.

✦ CONCLUSION ✦

In the same way I put up with suffering to cure a disease, I am going to deal patiently with problems to cure the disease of anger and its imprints.

✦ DEDICATION ✦

A Meditation on the Clear-Light Nature of the Conventional Mind

Thubten Tsultrim (George Churinoff)

The meditation I have found most useful through the years is one introduced to me by my kind guru, Lama Yeshe. I call this a meditation on the clear light nature of the conventional mind, and I find it a great inspiration. It reminds me of our potential to remove all harmful states of mind and replace them, in the clarity of our minds, with wholesome states such as compassion and wisdom. Some great teachers, such as His Holiness the Dalai Lama, actually refer to this clarity of the mind as the conventional buddha potential (the actual buddha potential is said to be the ultimate nature of the mind, its emptiness). This meditation helps to lift the depressed mind, and to quiet and concentrate the troubled mind. It prepares us to meditate on emptiness and, as well, is a superb preparation for tantric visualization.

The meditation itself is drawn from the experiences of the great yogis of the past, especially those from the Mahamudra tradition. All our experiences are conditioned by our mental state. We are constantly engaged in a mental conversation of which we are unaware, and we respond to various events out of our subjective judgments, which are often erroneous and harmful. I like to say that this meditation helps us familiarize ourselves with the laboratory of the mind. In this laboratory we can observe these disturbing factors and can perform the great spiritual experiments that were done by the great masters of the past.

✦ PRELIMINARIES ✦

The actual meditation requires a good degree of concentration and subtlety of mind, so I find it useful to begin with meditation on the breath as an aid in bringing the mind to such a state. Sit comfortably with the back erect and focus on the breath as though you were asked to listen to it—that is, without trying to control it or judge it: "Oh, that was a good one!"

Watch the breath as it comes in, pauses, goes out, pauses, comes in, and so on. Focus particularly at the end points, where the mind has the tendency to be lazy and occupy itself with fantasies or other thoughts. Put all your mental energy into concentration and simply ignore other thoughts that might tempt you: just let the thoughts go by.

If you are beginning such practice, you might find that mentally counting the cycles of respiration (i.e., this is the first inhalation, now it is changing direction, this is the first exhalation...) will help you notice and let go of distracting thoughts. It is like having both your hands full and being offered a cup of tea—there is no way to take it unless you give up one of the objects in your hands.

✦ THE MEDITATION ✦

When the mind has become somewhat focused, follow one inhalation up the nostrils, down to the area of the heart chakra, and away from the head, the area more associated with conceptual thought. Place your attention on the mind itself instead of on the respiration. Remind yourself that you are not paying attention to the other five senses, but to the sixth sense, the mental consciousness.

Spend some time at first observing the thoughts and images that are constantly flowing through the mind. Just observe the thoughts without getting involved with them. It is like when you are sitting at a streetside cafe watching the people passing by; one just notes them but does not get up and follow them down the street. Try to get familiar with the laboratory of the mind.

Try to notice the quiet moments between thoughts and focus on those as you previously focused on the breath. Then, whenever a thought arises and distracts you from focusing on the clear quiet nature of the mind, let go of your attention to that objective thought and refocus your attention on the subjective mind within which the thought is appearing, the clear quiet nature of the mind itself.

The Buddha and the great practitioners after him have said that the nature of the mind is clear light: nonmaterial, unobstructed by thoughts, and posing no obstruction to them. Try to focus your attention on this clear-light nature of the mind within which all mental events occur. The mind can be likened to an ocean, and the thoughts and other mental events to fish swimming through that clear medium.

We are ordinarily unaware of the nature of the mind and instead observe only the fish-like thoughts. It is as though we were observing an aquarium through a large glass wall and at first only noticed the fish. If someone were to tell us to observe the clear water within which the fish were swimming, we might at first have difficulty noticing it because of its transparency. But by simply realizing that the fish could not be moving unless there was some substance to move in, we can take our attention away from observing the fish and focus instead on the clear water.

In a similar fashion, try again and again to let go of attention to the fish-like thoughts and try to recognize the clear-light nature of the mind within which all mental events occur. In the case of the aquarium, the fish will remain before us when we focus on the water. However, when we focus our attention on the clear-light nature of the mind, the thoughts begin to diminish in intensity and frequency, thereby quieting the mind and enhancing our ability to concentrate.

✦ DEDICATION ✦

A Meditation
on the Body of Light

Sangye Khadro (Kathleen McDonald)

✦ INTRODUCTION ✦

This meditation was devised as an introduction to deity practice. One visualizes that a buddha figure such as Shakyamuni Buddha, Chenrezig, or Tara dissolves into oneself, becoming oneness, and then sends light to all beings to benefit them. Some people find it difficult to visualize deities, or even to relate to them due to cultural differences. I feel this simplified visualization contains the essence of deity practice—getting in touch with one's innate good qualities and buddha nature. It could be practiced on its own, or as a way of training oneself in visualization techniques before going on to more complex meditations, such as the visualization of the Buddha.

✦ PRELIMINARIES ✦

Sit comfortably with your back straight. Let your body relax; let go of any tension you may have in your body—imagine that the tension melts, dissolves, and flows away, leaving your body relaxed, light, and free from tension. Let your breath flow in and out naturally. Have the thought or motivation that you are doing this meditation in order to become a kinder, wiser person, better able to help others.

✦ THE MEDITATION ✦

When your mind is calm and clear, visualize in the space above your head a sphere of white light somewhat smaller than the size of your head. It is made of pure light, transparent and radiant. Spend several minutes concentrating on the light, feeling its presence above your head. Don't worry if it does not appear sharply; it is enough just to feel it is there.

Contemplate that the sphere of light represents all good qualities that exist. Bring to mind the good qualities you admire in others and would like to have within yourself: selflessness, love, compassion, generosity, patience, wisdom, humility, and so forth; and think that this light is the essence of these qualities. You can also think that it represents your own highest potential to be free of everything negative and to perfect everything positive, in other words, your buddha nature.

Then visualize that the sphere of light decreases in size until it is about one inch in diameter, and it descends through the top of your head to your heart chakra in the center of your chest. From there it begins to expand once more, slowly spreading to fill your entire body. As it does, all the solid parts of your body dissolve and become light—your organs, bones, blood vessels, tissue, and skin all become pure, transparent white light. Your body becomes a body of light.

Concentrate on the experience of your body being a body of light. Think that all the good qualities represented by the light—love, compassion, wisdom, and so forth—have become part of you; you are these qualities. Feel that all problems, negative energy, obstacles, and limitations have completely vanished and that you have reached a state of wholeness and perfection. Feel serene and joyful. If any thought or distracting object appears in your mind, imagine that it also dissolves into white light. Meditate in this way for several minutes.

After some time, generate the wish to share this experience with others. Visualize that rays of light radiate from your heart, going out through all the pores of your body into every direction, just as light radiates from the sun. These rays go to each and every being in the universe and fill them with light. All these beings become free of all their problems and negativities and are filled with positive energy. Their bodies dissolve into pure light, and their minds experience peace and bliss. Meditate on this for some time, and feel joyful that you have been able to help all beings in this way.

✦ DEDICATION ✦

When you wish to end the meditation, mentally dedicate the merit, or positive energy, from doing the meditation to the benefit of yourself and all other beings, helping all beings to become free from confusion and problems, to reach a state of peace and perfection, the state of enlightenment.

A Meditation on Checking the "I"

Jamyang Wangmo (Helly Pelaez Bozzi)

+ INTRODUCTION +

Let us consider what we mean by meditation. The Tibetan terms usually translated as "meditation" are *gom* and *nyamshag*. *Gom* means becoming habituated, and *nyamshag* means resting in a state of harmony or equanimity. Now let's become accustomed to resting in a harmonious state of mind. In order to achieve mental harmony, the gross and subtle elements—earth, water, fire, air, and space—which constitute our body, must also be in harmony. Sitting in a proper position and breathing correctly are extremely important for harmonizing our body and mind.

+ PRELIMINARIES +

Begin the meditation session either by making three prostrations to the Buddha, the Dharma, and the Sangha in order to purify your body, speech, and mind; or begin by prostrating to each buddha of the five directions—east, south, west, north, and center—and to each of the female buddhas of the five intermediate directions. The first five prostrations are to purify the five aggregates and the second five are to purify the five elements.

Sit properly in the posture of Buddha Vairochana; pay special attention to keeping your back very straight. Do not close your eyes; closing

77

your eyes helps to isolate you from the external objects and environment, but meditation does not mean sitting on your own cloud ignoring the world around you. Meditation means being truly and harmoniously in the world, flowing with it instead of ignoring it.

Recite the refuge and bodhichitta prayers and pray to the lama by saying:

"Lama, please pay attention to me! Lama, please understand my problems and needs!"

Recite this many times to reaffirm the spiritual connection with your teacher. Whether or not your flesh-and-blood spiritual master can actually hear you is something difficult to know. But you will certainly be able to connect with the stream of pure enlightened energy of which the physical form of the lama is a vehicle.

Open your heart to the enlightened energy of your lama. Don't do anything else with your mind.

✦ THE MEDITATION ✦

When you feel your whole body and mind imbued with the lama's blessings, watch your breath and count twenty-one sets of inhalations and exhalations. If you get distracted, start again from the beginning.

Reflect upon the great value and usefulness of your precious human body. Recite the mantra of Amitayus or White Tara or any other mantra for longevity, and think:

"I did not take a human body in order to waste my life in meaningless, useless, or harmful activities. I was born human in order to progress on the spiritual path and to help others do the same. At least today I will do something beneficial and useful, and I will not waste my time. Who knows whether this time tomorrow I will still be alive? Today could be my last chance!"

Observe your mind. Let the thoughts come and go. Do not interfere with their flow; do not identify yourself with them. Do not consciously think; just let thoughts and mental images flow freely. When you ignore thoughts, there is no energy to sustain them, so they will eventually disappear by themselves.

When the storm of your thoughts and mental images has subsided, be aware of your sense of self and check:

Who am I?

Where am I?

With what do I identify?

You may get caught up again by desire, anger, jealousy, pride, and so forth. Do not identify yourself with them. They are just conceptuality.

"Conceptual thoughts, images, and feelings are not me, are not my real self."

"What about my body, made up of the five elements; can I identify myself with it? Can I identify myself with each one of the elements separately or with the combination of them?"

After some time of practicing continuously in this way, you may reach a conclusion:

"Logically speaking, I cannot identify myself with either the stream of thoughts and mental images or the five elements that constitute my body. I, my real self, must be something else."

Do not stop at that point. A logical conclusion is just another conceptual thought. Keep on watching your mind until you perceive something of the authentic nature of the mind: clarity, bliss, emptiness.

Realize that the authentic sense of "I" is arising dependent on just the clear light nature of mind, which is vast and blissful, like empty space.

Rest in that harmonious, blissful, empty clarity.

✦ DEDICATION ✦

Conclude the meditation session by imagining sharing this positive energy with everybody, particularly with those people who are in great need of bliss and clarity because of physical or mental problems.

Recite dedication prayers such as the "King of Prayers" and make good wishes for the long life of the spiritual teachers and for the pure Dharma to exist a long time without adulteration. Pray to again receive a human body and circumstances conducive to Dharma practice. Pray to be able to meet realized spiritual masters, to study the Dharma, and to obtain a level of spiritual development that would enable you to help many sentient beings.

Stand up, stretch your legs and arms, drink your coffee, tea, fruit juice, or whatever, and start your daily activities with a calm and happy mind. In the midst of the endless show of human madness, endeavor to maintain the awareness of who we all are: blissful clear light and emptiness, that's all.

A Meditation on Dependent Arising and Emptiness

Thubten Kunsel (Robina Courtin)

✦ INTRODUCTION ✦

According to Lord Buddha, all our sufferings and fears are rooted in our deeply held and utterly irrational belief in solid, real things existing out there, in and of themselves, independent of everything else. As Lama Zopa Rinpoche says, we live in a world "made up by our own minds." This delusional way of seeing the world—and ourselves—is so pervasive that initially it's impossible to detect.

Lama Tsongkhapa says that the most skillful way to loosen the grip of this fantasy, and to eventually bring our minds into sync with how things actually are—and thus eradicate suffering and fear—is to contemplate dependent arising. As Lama Yeshe says, it's "the king of logic to prove emptiness"—to prove, in other words, that things are empty of, or lack, the type of existence that our hallucinating minds think they have.

✦ PRELIMINARIES ✦

✦ THE MEDITATION ✦

Take this body of ours. It's what we believe in most as something real from its own side; it's what we cling to most, think about most, take care of most, identify with most. To our hallucinating minds, it's the one thing that is definitely "me."

But think: how is it "my body"? It has come into being, and continues to exist, in dependence upon countless causes and conditions. We cannot find "my body" among any one of those causes and conditions, yet it is nothing other than those causes and conditions.

As Geshe Jampa Tegchok says, "It can be said that everything in the universe before [this body] came into being is a valid cause and condition for the existence of [this body]."

Think: My body began with the egg and sperm of my kind mother and father (thank you Mother and Father!). So, where is "my body"?

Without the mother and father's parents, there would be no mother and father; and without mother and father, there would be no "my body."

Where is my body apart from these beginningless mothers and fathers?

Without my mother's womb, the egg and sperm could not join and develop. Without the food my mother ate every day, the egg and sperm could not grow into a fetus.

Where is my body apart from the food she ate?

My body is nothing other than a mountain of carrots and potatoes and chickens and bread. Without the earth, the gardener, the sun, the water, the fertilizer, there would be no carrots; without the carrots there would be no mother; without my mother, there could be no "my body." It does not exist.

My body would not exist without the clothes my mother wore to keep her warm in the winter; the clothes would not exist without the sheep who provided the wool, the sheep shearers, the sheep shearers' mothers, the owners of the sheep, the people who processed the wool, the people who turned it into cloth, the truck drivers who took the cloth to the clothes factory, the clothes designers, the tailors, the sewing machines, the designers of the sewing machines, the shops that sold the clothes, the people who made the racks the clothes hung on...

Where is my body apart from these? It cannot be found.

My body would not exist without the cotton bushes, the people who planted the cotton, the gardeners who nourished the cotton bushes, the people who picked the cotton, the people who drove the trucks that took the cotton to be processed, the architect of the factory where the cotton was turned into cloth, the people who turned the cotton into cloth, the people who dyed the cloth, the people who made the dye, the person who designed the packet that contained the dye, the printer who printed the packet, the people who made the printing machine...

Where is my body apart from all of these causes and conditions? It does not exist.

My body would not exist without the doctors and nurses who helped it come out of the womb, the soft cloth that protected it and kept it warm, the cot in which it was put to sleep, the milk from my mother's breasts, the food that my mother ate that transformed into the milk that nourished my body, the nurses who checked the body while it was sleeping to make sure it did not suffocate, the heating in the hospital that kept the body warm, the electricity that kept the heaters burning, the electricians who did the wiring in the hospital, the colleges they went to to learn to become electricians, the teachers of the electricians...

Where is my body apart from all these countless causes and conditions? It cannot be found anywhere.

My body is nothing other than all the food I ate as a child: the milk and rice and peas and lamb and apples and eggs; my body would not exist without the food, the gardeners, the people who trucked the vegetables to the market, the people who sold the vegetables, the people who made the shelves at the market that held the vegetables off the ground, the people who made the stalls at the market, the people who made the shop where they sold the lamb, the person who killed the lamb, the lamb's mother, the people who skinned the lamb, the person who packed it, the person who put it in the refrigerator at the supermarket, the people who made the refrigerator, the people who made the factory where the refrigerator was made...

Where is my body apart from all this?

My body would not exist without the mountains of morality practiced in a previous life that is its main karmic cause; the morality could not have been practiced without the kindness of the gurus who showed the path to the person in the previous life, without the kindness of the Dharma friends, the books in which the Dharma was printed, the people who printed the Dharma books, the person who designed the typeface used in the Dharma books, the people who made the paper, the people who chopped down the trees from which the paper was made, the previous parents, the food the previous mother ate to nourish her body so that the body in her womb could grow, so that the previous person could survive to practice morality in order to create the cause to have my body in this life...

It is clear that there is no "my body" apart from these beginningless causes and conditions. So what is there to cling to?

✦ CONCLUSION ✦

Now, convinced that this body of ours is empty of even an atom of self-existence, pray to become like the bodhisattva for whom, as Kirti Tsenshab Rinpoche says, the action of "cutting off their hand to feed a starving animal is as inconsequential as a leaf falling off a tree."

✦ DEDICATION ✦

THE NUNS AND MONKS

Tenzin Tsapel
(Gillian Jelbart)

I was born in Melbourne, Australia, in 1953 to kind and loving parents. I am the fourth of four girls with a younger brother. We had many happy times with a large circle of cousins and friends and with uncles and aunts to visit in the country. I was an average student interested in creative activities and also the pressing social issues of the 1960s—nuclear disarmament, the peace movement, the environment, aboriginal rights, and others. However, I felt quite powerless and I worried that adults had so few answers. I qualified in architectural drafting at Melbourne Institute of Technology and enjoyed drafting and design work as a young adult. At twenty-three I designed and helped build a mud house with friends in rural Victoria. It was there I met a student of the lamas who lent me a copy of *Wisdom Energy*, which inspired me to attend Lama Zopa Rinpoche's 1979 Lamrim course at Chenrezig Institute. Rinpoche and Lama Yeshe were the most extraordinary people I had ever met, and I became a Buddhist at that stage, taking refuge with Lama Yeshe.

I continued to study with Geshe Dawo at Tara Institute in Melbourne and went to India in 1982 for the Enlightened Experience Celebration. While there I also did a Vajrasattva group retreat and a month of solitary retreat. It was a very happy year that I feel laid the foundation for my later leanings toward ordination. The wish for ordination surfaced six months after my return during a visit of Lama Zopa Rinpoche. Though it had seemed logical, this was the first time that ordination appeared as an attractive option. The idea filled with me pleasure and surprise, but I suspected it to have a fleeting nature. The desire stayed with me and brought peace and happiness, so with Rinpoche's permission and guidance I was ordained by His Holiness the Dalai Lama in Bodhgaya in February 1985.

I feel very lucky to be ordained; I've had many happy times and feel committed to the process of inner war on the afflictions and the self-cherishing attitude. I've had time for several solitary and group retreats and have enjoyed combining study with teaching. I joined the Chenrezig Nuns Community in 1991, and I've been able to use my design and building skills for their benefit. My major interests now are to continue to study with Geshe Tashi Tsering, to assist the Chenrezig Nuns Community, and to help with the wider work of Chenrezig Institute and the FPMT.

Chenrezig Institute
Queensland, Australia

Jampa Shenphen
(Jesus Revert)

My name is Jampa Shenphen, and I was born in Onteniente, Spain, in 1958. Although I knew something about Tibetan Buddhism and had read some books, I was not interested in it until I met Geshe Lobsang Tsultrim at O.Sel.Ling, a retreat center in the south of Spain, in 1982. I was living there, working as a gardener. I liked the place and the people, and had decided to stay for a short while. The presence of Geshe-la—his words and advice, his kindness and peace of mind—was so inspiring that I felt I had much to learn from him, and the best thing I could do in my life was to follow his advice and his example.

From the moment I met him until today, Geshe Tsultrim has always been my guide, my refuge and protector, and the faith I had in him the very first day we met has only become stronger and more stable during all these years. Following Geshe-la's advice, I went to study Tibetan language and Buddhist philosophy at Rabten Choeling Monastery in Switzerland, where I took novice ordination from its abbot, Geshe Rabten.

When I decided to become a monk I had many doubts and fears. I thought I would be unable to keep the vows and discipline and feared that I might remain ordained only for a short period of time. But a few months after taking ordination and living in the monastery I started to feel very happy and comfortable with my new life. I realized that, as a monk, I had much better conditions to practice Dharma, and I was much more protected from obstacles and distractions. The monastic routine and duties also became something that gave order and freedom to my mind. Now, having experienced more than fifteen years of monastic life, the normal life of a person living in a city, having a job, family, social life, and so forth, appears as something quite difficult and complicated, without any order or freedom, and as something I would not like to have to live with. I studied with Geshe Rabten for three years. In 1988, I moved to Barcelona, where I stayed with my teacher and worked as a translator at Nagarjuna Centre.

In January 1991 I joined Sera-Je Monastery in South India to continue the Geshe studies I had already begun in Switzerland. At present, ten years later, I am in the Madyamika class, and I hope to be able to complete the whole Geshe program. The first four or five years in the monastery were quite difficult because I had to push myself very hard with the studies and debates to be able to keep pace with my classmates. But for the last three years I have very much enjoyed reading the texts and my studies. I think this is a result of the hard work I have done. In 1998 I finally received full ordination from His Holiness the Dalai Lama. I feel very fortunate to be able to live and study in Sera. I don't have any specific plans for the future, and I only hope that my life becomes beneficial for others.

Sera-Je Monastery
Bylakuppe, India

Yeshe Choedzom
(Margaret McAndrew)

I was born in Australia in 1944, and up to the age of twenty-one, I lived in small country towns while dreaming of being able to travel. Eventually I moved to Melbourne where I gained a librarianship diploma in 1972. During this time I took a year off and traveled to Europe, but it was my brief contact with a few Asian destinations on the way back—especially three days in Delhi—that made the greatest impression on me, and I couldn't wait to go back. Meanwhile I had a normal life, boyfriends, and many interests, including cooking, skiing, and bushwalking. But I was very unhappy, unsettled, and discontented. I could not imagine marrying and settling down.

In 1973, at the age of twenty-nine, I set out to travel through Southeast Asia to India. Out of my interest in mythology I had already begun to feel some interest in Eastern religions in general. This led me to visit many Buddhist temples, and I also met a number of Western travelers who had become practicing Buddhists, a new phenomenon at that time. I began to feel that Buddhism had something special to offer, and I hoped meditation might help me with my unhappy and discontented mind—the monks always seemed so peaceful! But I certainly wasn't looking for a "religion," having found the Anglican faith of my childhood unsatisfying.

In India I started to encounter Tibetan Buddhism. I went to Bodhgaya to attend a vipassana course just as His Holiness the Dalai Lama came to give the Kalachakra initiation to thousands of Tibetans. I was fascinated but overwhelmed by all the color and activity. However I made contacts that led me to taking one of the month-long Kopan Monastery courses in Nepal in the spring of 1974.

During that course I found I had a strong connection with the two lamas and the Graduated Path, which provided the answers I had been looking for without knowing it. I was unbelievably happy when I found this wonderfully practical, inspiring, and compassionate path. From then on I wanted to devote my life to following Buddha's teachings in as strong a way as possible. After a couple of years I thought it might be best to become a nun, as I was afraid of being drawn back into the meaningless activities of my old way of life. Eleven other people had the same idea at the same time. I took rabjung vows in December 1975 and getsul vows from Trijang Rinpoche in April 1976 with Thubten Gyatso, Roger Kunsang, and others. Owing to visa problems we were always on the move, spending much of the year in India, doing retreats or studying at the Tibetan Library at Dharamsala, and then returning to Nepal for the winter to be with our lamas. Eventually money ran out and I came back to Australia, sick, broke, and suffering from reverse culture shock. I didn't get better quickly, and those first years were quite a struggle as we new inexperienced Buddhists tried to get centers going and gain public acceptance. After two years helping the director of Tara Institute in Melbourne, I was advised by Lama Yeshe to move to Chenrezig Institute, where I worked as the cook for my keep. By the miracle of Lama's blessing I was able to attend the first Enlightened Experience Celebration held in India in 1981 and 1982 in spite of my woeful financial situation.

I came back in debt, so it was back to Melbourne to earn money by caring for elderly people, and to save enough to carry out Lama's instructions to go to Dorje Pamo Nunnery in France. Then came the sad news of Lama Yeshe's death, so I joined the last nine months of the year-long Vajrasattva retreat held at Kopan for Lama. Reluctantly I went to France. I never wanted to leave India, but it was a valuable experience to be involved in the little community of nuns living in the farm buildings of an old chateau. I also attended His Holiness the Dalai Lama's Kalachakra initiation at Rikon in Switzerland. I returned to Nepal for the second Enlightened Experience Celebration and then back to Australia, and finally to Chenrezig Institute where a few of us started the Chenrezig Nuns community. I have been more or less settled there ever since, with some longish breaks in Adelaide at Buddha House, and in Taipei.

Over the years I have been fortunate in receiving teachings from many lamas besides my chief teachers, Lama Yeshe and Lama Zopa Rinpoche. I have also been able to make various retreats including a strict five-month deity retreat, my longest to date. In spite of my advantages I am not much of either a scholar or a meditator, but I am a practical person who is happiest working at my gurus' centers.

It has been fantastic to see the development of Dharma in Australia. I would never have believed it possible when we were starting off in the seventies. My dream always was to see a nuns' community established in Australasia, and now Chenrezig Nuns Community seems to be developing strongly. Thanks to an inheritance I now have a comfortable little unit there, and my financial and health problems have eased a lot. But they have given me an understanding of the difficulties still faced by the majority of Western Sangha. My dearest wish is to see a situation where nuns and monks are supported in their practice and in return act as spiritual assets to the wider community. I hope in the future that new nuns will be able to reach a level of training and development in a few years that we old nuns have hardly been able to reach in twenty years. It seems, due to the kindness of our lamas and the generosity and hard work of many people, that this is starting to come about.

Chenrezig Institute
Queensland, Australia

Thubten Dondrub
(Neil Huston)

I was born in Adelaide, Australia, in 1947. For the first part of my life I had no interest in religion, meditation, or what happened after death. I saw economic equality and political justice as the keys to solving the world's problems. I didn't want to be part of those problems, but I didn't know how to be part of the solution. After graduating from university I moved to Sydney where I worked as a teacher and in other jobs, all of which I found boring and strangely disillusioning. Around 1973, after breaking up with my girlfriend, I moved to the countryside of northern New South Wales convinced that the meaning of life could be found in living a simple, alternative lifestyle.

After three years of that, things were looking grim, so I enrolled at the local teachers college. The course was another big disappointment and by the Easter holidays I was desperate. A good friend had attended the first course that Lama Yeshe and Lama Zopa Rinpoche had taught at Diamond Valley in 1974. As a result he had gone to live at Chenrezig Institute in Queensland when it first opened in 1975. I received a letter from him saying that he was having doubts about Buddhism. With nothing to do over the Easter holidays I resolved to rescue him from the clutches of this cult. We could go off to some beach where I could work out the next step of my life.

I arrived unannounced at the Institute as my friend was working on putting down the floor of a new building. He stepped back in surprise; the floorboard flew up, and nearly gouged his eye out. I drove him off to the doctor to get some stitches, and on the way discovered that he had resolved his doubts about Buddhism. I had nowhere to go and felt that I couldn't leave anyway, having been responsible for his almost losing an eye. So I spent my ten-day holiday at Chenrezig Institute following the expected discipline of attendance at morning and evening meditation, and helping with the work. There were no teachings, but we discussed ideas over lunch. The concept of mind and its potential really appealed to me, and somehow most of what I heard seemed to echo what I had felt but had never been able to articulate, or synthesize before.

When I returned home, I discovered to my surprise that I was happy, that life had meaning, and that I wanted to learn more about Buddhism. I dropped out of the college course and went to live at a small Buddhist community nearby. I went back to Chenrezig Institute to attend the month-long meditation course given by Lama Zopa Rinpoche and Lama Yeshe in June 1976. I hadn't imagined that such a being as Lama Zopa Rinpoche could exist, and the teachings were so powerful and moving. Somehow, as the course progressed, I felt that I should become a monk. Fortunately I was advised to wait some time to see how I felt.

I went back to live at the small Buddhist community where I spent ten of the happiest months of my life before going back to Chenrezig Institute to do a retreat. Again during the retreat I felt a strong wish to get ordained. There were almost no Western monks or nuns around at that time, so I really had no clear idea of what it meant to be ordained or how I would live. I just saw no alternative. Everything in my life seemed to be bringing me to this point. I didn't want to be part of the business world or the education system. I hadn't found the right person to live with, which before meeting the Dharma had meant a lot of loneliness; but after meeting Buddhism I immediately felt some sense of inner contentment and self-reliance. And I did want to give meaning to my life by helping others, or at least by not harming them. In March 1977 I took the rabjung vows and in June 1977 was part of a group of seven men who took novice ordination. This was the first time it was ever granted in Australia. Lama Yeshe came from New Zealand to Australia just to take part in the ceremony, making up the required number of ordaining monks. In 1979 I was incredibly fortunate to receive full ordination from Lama Zopa Rinpoche with Lama Yeshe as one of the ordaining monks and acting as "time-keeper."

I lived at Chenrezig Institute from 1977 until 1981 and was fortunate to receive many wonderful teachings from Geshe Thubten Loden and other masters. Lama Yeshe then asked me to accompany Geshe Legden, abbot of Sera-Je Monastery, on a tour of the FPMT centers in Europe. At the end of it, I accompanied the abbot back to Sera-Je Monastery in South India, where I stayed for a year trying to learn Tibetan. A letter came from Lama Yeshe asking me to be Lama Zopa Rinpoche's attendant for the coming 1983 tour. I very happily accepted. By this stage the work of Lama Yeshe and Rinpoche had increased so much that each needed a full-time secretary, so I remained as Rinpoche's attendant after the tour finished. Then very sadly Lama Yeshe died and Rinpoche had to take over the full burden of the FPMT. The years 1984 and 1985 were incredibly busy, amazing times spent with Lama Zopa Rinpoche, and crowned by the opportunity to receive many teachings and initiations from Rinpoche and His Holiness the Dalai Lama. I wearily resigned in 1986. In 1987 I was among over forty students who went with Rinpoche to Tibet, and at the end of that year I taught the November Course at Kopan Monastery.

The years from 1988 until early 1991, at Lama Zopa Rinpoche's request, I spent in Taipei, Taiwan trying to establish a center. It was one of the most difficult times of my life, only relieved by the incredible kindness I received from the group of students who became the heart of the new center. I then moved to Nalanda Monastery and from there became involved in teaching tours of Spain, Italy, America, and Australia. As well I taught the November Kopan Courses from 1996 until 1998. I am still based at Nalanda and teach at various FPMT centers around the world. In this way I hope I am able to repay something of the incomparable kindness and the inconceivable gift of Dharma that I have received from Lama Thubten Zopa Rinpoche and Lama Yeshe.

Nalanda Monastery
Lavaur, France

Losang Dekyong
(Angeles de la Torre)

I was born in Alicante, Spain, in 1940. I am the second of four children. My parents were very generous people, honest and well educated, with a great sense of humor, loving above all culture and spiritual values. Like most girls in Spain at that time, I went to a Catholic primary school staffed by nuns. I have a nice memory of it. I attended university in Madrid, studying philosophy for three years, but it didn't fill my expectations of how philosophy could help my life. I went to Barcelona to study classical languages thinking this linguistic method would help my disorganized mind. I also became very involved in politics. When I finished my studies I taught linguistics at a secondary school and then at the university. But my life wasn't happy. Seeking psychological balance I did psychoanalysis for some years. I didn't agree at all with the political situation in Spain at that time, so with no other thought in mind, when Nehru University in Delhi requested a teacher of Spanish, I took the chance to escape Spain.

The first people I met in Delhi were a French couple who were very interested in Buddhism, and it was from them that I first heard about the Buddha and about lamas. During a holiday we went to Dharamsala. At Namgyal Monastery the monks were debating, and I was completely surprised when I realized it wasn't a dance but a way to learn how to reason properly in order to live correctly. I thought that a culture that had developed such a way of learning should be very interesting, and I began studying Buddhism. My friends knew one of Lama Yeshe's students who was always encouraging them to go to Kopan Monastery to do a meditation course. I decided to go.

In the beginning everything was strange, and I didn't agree with anything. The first teaching was by Kyabje Song Rinpoche. I didn't understand a thing. I felt absolutely ridiculous prostrating, reciting strange words, and sitting on the floor for long periods. I wanted to leave but went instead to the teachings of a very young lama. He was talking about the mind, "The mind is beginningless..." I was completely shocked. I felt a door start to open. All month my mind was working hard, increasing each day my interest in the teachings. I attended the Kopan Course three more times.

After one of the courses, Lama Yeshe asked me to take a statue to one of his gurus in Delhi. I went to visit Kyabje Ling Rinpoche to offer the statue, thinking it was for him. I had a wonderful meeting with Kyabje Ling Rinpoche, who invited me to have tea. During the tea, smiling, he told me, "You are wrong. This statue is for..." and he pronounced a very strange name. The next day I went to meet the other lama, who was Kyabje Trijang Rinpoche. When I went into his room I felt his smile go directly to my heart and I started to cry; but I felt happy! It was a kind of happiness I had never experienced before. I was invited to lunch the next day, and the next day, and the next day, too. Every day I had questions and every day I received the most incredible Dharma teachings. He asked me, "Do you know what statue you brought?" I didn't. He said: "This is a Namgyalma statue. Do you know what it means and the meaning of guru devotion?" That was the beginning of my life. It was around January 1974. I don't think I ever thanked Lama Yeshe enough times for putting me on the way to finding my root guru.

After that encounter I started to think more about what direction I wanted my life to take. For the first time I felt absolutely alive; I had a purpose, a goal. I knew I wanted to follow the same direction as my guru, and to become like him in order to be able to help others. I understood I was on the way to achieving the happiness I had been looking for all my life. I decided to dedicate my life to developing the state of mind able to help other sentient beings. I decided to get ordained.

I was ordained in April 1976 at Tushita Retreat Centre in Dharamsala. I was ordained by Kyabje Trijang Dorje Chang. The translator was Lama Zopa Rinpoche. Lama Yeshe, Geshe Jampa Tegchok, and Geshe Ngawang Dhargyey were also present, but I don't remember who else. Since that time my life has been dedicated to study and to trying to practice according to the lineage of Lama Tsongkhapa. In 1977 I returned to Alicante for family reasons and became involved in private language tutoring, which often became mixed with counseling as well. I have continued this work up to the present. Through this, some people were attracted to the Dharma, and as a result, in 1998 Nagarjuna Centre started in Alicante. I teach at the Centre four nights a week and coordinate a group interested in developing a hospice service inspired by the Buddha's teachings.

I know I've been wrong many times because of not knowing how to be really free of my delusions. But I always know that the pure wisdom, pure love and compassion of my gurus is with me on the path, and that they will never abandon me, for they are my guides. I also know that, while I am alive, my body, speech, and mind will never stop following the Three Jewels, will never stop following the path my gurus showed with their pure example and vibrant teachings.

Nagarjuna C.E.T.
Alicante, Spain

Thubten Pemo
(Linda Grossman)

I was born into a Jewish family in 1947 in Brooklyn, New York. During the first years of my life, we lived with my grandmother, who was very strict in her religious observances. As a child, I enjoyed going to the rabbi's house and felt happy that the people were praying.

As a small child I sometimes saw children harming one another and found it unbearable. I thought that we should love and help everyone, and not give harm. So I made up my own rules for not harming people and lived according to my rules, which were: not to kill, steal, tell lies, drink alcohol, and so forth. Also as a child I wanted very much to be good and pure, and I wanted to meet someone who would teach me how. But I thought that such a person did not exist.

I was in college when my mother suddenly died of a heart attack. For the next years I lived alone and worked in New York City, continuing my college classes at night. One day I discovered the word "wisdom" and did not know what it was, but I was interested in having it. I read the list of all the subjects taught in my college and it was all "book learning." No one was teaching "wisdom." I wanted so much to have wisdom that I stopped going to college. I continued working but felt that my life had no real meaning. I was not very happy and thought that traveling to other countries seeing beautiful places and people might bring some happiness. So in 1969 when my friend Florence said she was going to the World's Fair in Japan, I decided to go with her. Even before leaving we kept adding more exotic destinations. One day Florence read about a country named Nepal, home of the Himalayas. I had never heard of Nepal but agreed to add it to our itinerary.

So it was that I landed in Kathmandu, Nepal in 1970. I made my way up Kopan Hill through the advice of some Australians we met. They told me there was a Tibetan lama giving a lecture and that he was a "together-with-it man." I didn't know what a together-with-it man was and had never met one in New York. Also, I thought that after going to this lecture, I could tell people back home that I had met a Tibetan lama during my travels.

With this worldly motivation I went to my first Buddhist teaching, given by Lama Thubten Yeshe at Kopan in 1970. I did not understand most of what Lama Yeshe said but was very moved just looking at his body and watching him speak. I thought, "This is the nicest man I've ever met, and I want to be like him." In the spring of 1971 I trekked up to Lawudo and visited Lama Thubten Zopa Rinpoche in his cave. Rinpoche very kindly gave me my first Buddhist book to read. I did not understand it, so I read it three times. Leaving Lawudo ten days later, the thought arose, "Oh, I will become a nun and live in the Himalayas." But still I did not know what Buddhism was.

After two years of traveling, I returned to New York to earn money so that I could go back to live in Nepal and study with Lama Yeshe and Lama Zopa Rinpoche. Reading books on Buddhism back home, I felt that I had finally found a religion or philosophy that agreed with me! Here, at last, were teachings on loving-kindness, compassion, wisdom, and a path to goodness and perfection. I had found what I was searching for. While working in New York, I kept thinking about becoming a nun. I thought that first I would travel around the world and do everything I wanted for ten years, and then I would become a nun at age thirty-five. It seemed like a good age to settle down. I returned to Kopan Monastery for the November Meditation Course of 1973. During that course, which began on the anniversary of my mother's death, Lama Zopa Rinpoche kept talking about impermanence and death, especially about how we can die at any time. This led me to think, "I might not live to be thirty-five years old, and then I would die without becoming a nun." When the meditation course ended, I took vows along with nine other Westerners. We went to Bodhgaya in India to receive the Kalachakra Initiation from His Holiness the Dalai Lama. When it ended, His Holiness cut off the last pieces of our hair, and Yongdzin Ling Rinpoche very kindly bestowed the novice vows. It was January of 1974.

Why did I become a nun? I could have remained in New York in a comfortable apartment, continued to work and attend teachings in my free time. But I wanted to reduce distractions and give my whole life to the study and practice of the Buddhadharma. I wished to live in Nepal, study with Lama and Rinpoche, and practice fully—day and night. I was not satisfied with going to Dharma teachings only a few days of the year.

For the next few years, the new Western monks and nuns lived at Kopan where we had a Sangha community and studied and worked together. Lama Yeshe encouraged us to start teaching. To my amazement, Lama asked me to teach a one-month Kopan Course in March–April 1976—on two weeks notice! In this way, I became the first female to teach a Kopan Course. Lama was very happy and said, "My nuns can teach!" Thus began a new era of Western women giving Tibetan Buddhist teachings. During the next years, I taught at meditation courses in Nepal, Europe, and the United States, as well as the Kopan Courses of 1981 and 1989.

Because of visa restrictions, I spent almost twenty years "homeless," traveling between Nepal and India, occasionally attending Rinpoche's teachings in Europe, Australia, and America. For many years my home was Dharamsala, India, with several winters in Bodhgaya and Delhi. Much of this time was spent receiving thousands of hours of oral teachings from Tibetan teachers. Sometimes I participated in group retreats or engaged in solitary retreats in the Himalayas. I spent many years living in communities, learning how to get along with people and how to help and serve. During all these years, I've been trying to understand clearly the teachings of Tibetan Buddhism and to put them into practice. What do these words really mean? How do I practice this in my life as an American? In 1996, I moved to Land of Calm Abiding, a retreat center in California, in order to be alone and have more time and energy to put into study and meditation. After years of being ill in Nepal and India, I needed to be in a country with clean food and water. Now in 2001 my body is a little bit healthier and my mind is a little bit healthier. Some of the mental afflictions are not quite as strong as they were when I was younger. Even a little less anger or attachment makes the mind more peaceful. Virtuous thoughts cause joy in the mind.

Our work as Dharma practitioners is to subdue our own minds. This is not easy. It takes great effort over a long time. It is the most difficult work that anyone can do, yet the most worthwhile, meaningful, beneficial thing that we can do with our life. I still don't know very much about Buddhism, but I know that the Dharma is precious, vast, and profound. It is the way things are. There is so much to practice, to come closer and closer to enlightenment as much as we can in this lifetime. I don't know what my future holds, but my wish is to spend the rest of my life in retreat working on my mind—only coming out sometimes to receive teachings and advice. I feel the most beneficial way to practice and subdue my mind is in solitude, but this is not for everyone. Maybe you, dear reader, can practice well while living in the world. I wish you every success in your practice.

Land of Calm Abiding
Big Sur, California, U.S.A.

Thubten Chodron
(Cherry Green)

I was raised in a typical middle-class American community. Growing up during the Vietnam War influenced me considerably, and as a teenager I wondered, "Why am I alive? What is the meaning of life? If people want to live in peace, why are they killing each other to do so? Why is there prejudice against people based on their bodies—their skin color or their gender? What does it mean to love someone?"

I tried to find answers in the religious traditions available to me at the time, Judaism and Christianity, but was not satisfied by their responses. That an all-powerful creator God would create suffering and let it continue did not make sense to me. Neither did the story of creation. I had a scientific background, saw cause and effect work in the natural world, and was familiar with the concept of infinity. Thus a finite beginning to existence did not seem plausible to me. Some people told me to have faith and believe, but that left me cold. I had a questioning mind and felt that using our intelligence was important. Studying European history at the university, I noticed that for centuries, every generation experienced a war in the name of God and religion. I became disillusioned with organized religion and gave up seeking answers there, although my questions still remained.

In 1975, I was teaching in Los Angeles city schools and doing graduate work in education at the University of Southern California. Out of curiosity, I attended a three-week meditation course near Los Angeles taught by Lama Yeshe and Thubten Zopa Rinpoche. One of the first things the lamas said was, "You don't have to believe anything we say. Think about the Buddha's teachings. Try them out. Test them logically and see if they work in your own life." That open-minded approach agreed with me, so I listened to and checked out the teachings.

The Buddha's teachings that ignorance, anger, and attachment are the causes of suffering made an impact on me. I began to see how self-centered I was, and how these disturbing attitudes and emotions influenced almost everything I did. The teachings also spoke of our human potential, and the possibility of generating bodhichitta inspired me.

At the time I never thought of ordaining. I was married and loved my husband. Fortunately we didn't have children. However, as I looked deeper at my mind, I became concerned about my future lives. I had created so much negative karma in the past, and because my mind was so uncontrolled, I was creating so much more each day. I wondered how I could help anyone if I was born in the lower realms in the next life.

In addition, I saw that my ethical values were negotiable when it served my own selfish purposes. For example, I thought politicians' lying was horrible, but when I did not want others to know about something, my lying was okay. In fact, I rationalized that it was for the benefit of others, so they wouldn't be hurt. Seeing my tendency to bargain about ethical standards, I knew that I did not want to continue living that way the rest of my life. I had to make some firm, clear ethical decisions and then stick by them.

As I practiced more, my interest and trust in the Dharma grew, and I wanted Dharma practice to be the center of my life. But continuing in my busy life with career, studies, family, and social life made that very difficult. I needed to let go of other activities so that I would have more time to study and practice the Dharma.

For all these reasons—concern over future lives, wishing to live according to clear ethical standards, and wanting to dedicate my life to Dharma practice—I decided to request ordination. This was a surprise to me, as well as to those around me. If someone had asked me when I was twenty if I would ever be a Buddhist nun, I would have told them they were crazy. At that time, the idea of being celibate seemed ridiculous as well as impossible!

However, our lives often turn out differently than we plan, and in my case this was fortunate. Lama Yeshe had me wait nearly a year and a half from the time I requested ordination until the time of the ceremony, in 1977, with Kyabje Ling Rinpoche as my preceptor. Of course, I wanted to be ordained immediately, but Lama was wise to make me wait. I had to examine my motivation more closely and work through some difficult emotions, which certainly would have been an obstacle to my ordination had I been ordained immediately. For example, I had to let go of my attachment to my husband and my emotional dependence on the relationship. Meditation on impermanence helped with the former, learning to evaluate my own motivations and actions assuaged the latter. In addition, I had to deal with feelings of guilt because family members would be unhappy with my being a nun. Here, thought transformation practices helped me differentiate my responsibility from the responsibility of others for what they were feeling.

Now, when I meditate on death and look back on my life, I feel that receiving ordination was the best thing I did in this life. Not only did it put my energy in a good direction, it also acted as the basis for all further Dharma studies and practice. Since my ordination I have studied and worked as spiritual director at Istituto Lama Tzong Khapa in Italy and Dorje Pagmo Nunnery in France, and I was resident teacher at Amitabha Buddhist Centre in Singapore for a number of years. Currently I teach at the Dharma Friendship Foundation in Seattle and am active in improving the status and role of women in the Sangha. I pray to remain a nun and keep my precepts purely in this life and to be continuously ordained and live in pure precepts in future lives. I also pray that in this and all future lives the Sangha is worthy of respect and receives all the conditions necessary to practice, spread the Dharma, and benefit others.

Dharma Friendship Foundation
Seattle, U.S.A.

Losang Drimay
(Karen Gudmundsson)

I was born in 1960 to hard-working, responsible parents who made sure I had the advantages of good education, nutrition, life skills, and love. By inference, I know I did something right in past lives to have such good conditions this time. I grew up on the West Coast of the United States—California and Washington State—during an era of prosperity and in relatively peaceful surroundings. By the time I was a teenager, wanderlust overcame me, and by the generosity of my parents, I was able to have a number of experiences overseas, largely in Asia.

I received a bachelor's degree with a major in Asian Studies from a small, private school, University of Puget Sound, where a certain professor encouraged me in a career of contemplation, once suggesting to me the field of epistemology, or as he put it, "how we know what we know." This professor, who has kept in touch all these years, pointed out to us that in other parts of the world people believe that the whole community benefits from the meditating or praying of religious people. I remember thinking that that was a very different way of looking at things.

While pursuing higher studies, I came across a Dharma center in Vermont, Milarepa Center, which is part of the FPMT. Studying there was so different from what I had experienced in university settings because the lamas were teaching a living tradition that they were practicing as well. Instead of studying *about* Buddhism, I was suddenly able to study Buddhism itself. I was also encouraged by the warm welcoming I felt coming from the Tibetan lamas who not only said I could do it, but that I must do it...attain realizations on the path to enlightenment, that is. They never said I couldn't do it because of being a Westerner or a woman.

Since 1984, I have been living, working, and studying at various centers in the Gelug tradition, including a few years at the international office of the FPMT. What I have enjoyed about this kind of lifestyle is the variety of activities that fill my days. I get to do a little bit of everything: some physical work, some people work, all the while receiving teachings simply because I am involved with putting on the programs.

In 1991 I had the good fortune to take vows as a novice nun from Geshe Jampa Gyatso while visiting Istituto Lama Tzong Khapa in Italy. I had been thinking about becoming a nun for a few year already and even had a set of robes stashed away that one of my close teachers had given to me. But at that time, it was hard to get enough fully ordained monks together to perform the ceremony. My reasons for wanting to be a nun are not easily put into words, being more based on feeling than on logic. The effect, though, was that it brought my life into focus by making clear to my family and friends what I was doing and eliminating a lot of options that were making me feel pulled in different directions—alternate careers, relationships, and so forth.

Then in 1994, I participated in a full ordination ceremony at the International Buddhist Meditation Center in Los Angeles, California, together with several other nuns from our lineage, as well as people from other Buddhist traditions. What I liked about that experience was the completely international cooperation among the Buddhist Sangha, with ordaining masters and witnesses from all traditions. Curiously, both of my ordinations were conducted at least partly in English, with all the important points being translated, something that does not happen when people ordain in India or Nepal.

I had a few years off from this center work, due to the kindness of Lama Zopa Rinpoche, who let me live at our hermitage in San Simeon in order to spend more time on formal meditation and study. When Rinpoche told me to spend my final year there focusing on Lamrim, I felt that I was being sent to the back of the class. But with nothing else to do, I settled down to the assignment and came to appreciate the leisure that allowed me to become friends with that form of meditation. I had to use my own creativity in order to make the material meaningful to me. For example, I would rewrite the words into metered verse and draw pictures and diagrams that helped me see how different points connected to each other. Spending about a month on each topic, I looked more into the details than I ever would have normally.

Now I am back with my Dharma family at Vajrapani Institute, Boulder Creek, California, where the days bring me any sort of task that the center needs, from picking up a lama who is coming here to teach, to emptying the trash. Being in monastic robes, I am often thrust into ceremonial roles that I would not naturally be drawn to. I actually prefer to tinker with screws and wires and other solitary projects, but I have made an effort to overcome my insecurities and stand up in front of a group or lead a tune, trying to forget about how I look or sound. Whenever I get nervous, I recite the mantra, "It's not about me. It's not about me." I enjoy having philosophical conversations with people who are studying the same things as I am, and I even like talking to visitors about their lives, but I still have trouble being cheerful when people need a lot of things from me.

Recently, my efforts to remain unknown have started to unravel with Lama Zopa Rinpoche asking me to teach regular classes in Silicon Valley. Also, the growing number of new nuns in the area has put me in the position of mother hen, helping with orientations, getting the right kinds of clothing together, and running a sort of crisis hotline for the Sangha. Of course, sometimes I am the one having the crisis, so I am glad for the growing network of Western monks and nuns.

Vajrapani Institute
Boulder Creek, California, U.S.A.

Thubten Losang
(Tony Wengoborsky)

I was born in Berlin in 1949. Prior to encountering the Dharma, I had many, ultimately unfulfilling, experiences. These included being a Protestant Christian, atheist, communist, Trotskyite, militant anarchist, and hippie. In 1973 a friend, on his return from a trip to the East, introduced me to Buddhist ideas. I was immediately attracted to this new vision of life and I started studying Buddhist philosophy through whatever books were available at that time, and trying to live according to what I read. I considered myself a Buddhist though I really knew very little about it. In 1975 I also became very interested in alternative forms of farming as part of my evolving vision of how to live a good and meaningful life. While in Berlin a friend showed me an article in an underground magazine for the November Course at Kopan Monastery. It struck me as something very strict and serious, and just what I was looking for, so I decided to go.

The 1975 Kopan Course truly gave my life direction. I felt a very strong connection to both Lama Yeshe and Lama Zopa Rinpoche, the two teachers of the course, and to the teachings themselves. I was also impressed by the ordained disciples of the lamas. Even during the course it occurred to me as only logical that the best way to follow the Buddha's path was as a monk. After the course I did a two-and-a-half month Lamrim group retreat, at the end of which more than fifteen people took ordination. When I got back to Berlin I had completely changed. The changes were so positive that my mother became interested in the teachings and eventually took refuge and attended a number of teachings by Lama Yeshe. In 1976 I moved to Switzerland to undertake a training program in farming techniques. Each year I still managed to receive teachings from Lama Yeshe. In 1981 Lama Yeshe advised me that the best way to combine my Dharma practice with my interest in farming was to go to live at Vajrayogini Institute in France. I have been there ever since.

I went there wanting to have a family, but, after a number of failed relationships and observing the problems other people had in their personal lives, I saw this was not what I really wanted. At the same time I was beginning to find meditative life more interesting and satisfying. In 1988 I asked Lama Zopa Rinpoche what I had to do to live a life of meditation in solitude. Rinpoche's advice was that I get ordained. Although it took fourteen torturous years from the time I met the Dharma—and the enormously kind guidance of my teachers—for me to overcome the force of my mental afflictions and negative karma in order to take ordination, even in the 1975 Kopan Course I understood how beneficial ordination could be. For me it was an opening to a completely different approach to life. I saw in monasticism a set of very practical rules—a deliberately chosen, self-imposed framework for my mind (a bridle and harness if you will)—that offered a real and effective opportunity to definitely counteract and eliminate my afflictive emotions. At the same time I could see that ordination was a way to take a safe and meaningful direction in life.

When I took ordination my intention was to find the material and mental conditions to live, study, and meditate in solitude. However, I have not yet had the karma to achieve my goal to be a solitary meditator. During the first nine years of my stay at Vajrayogini Institute, I built up and took care of the grounds and gardens, but after being ordained as a novice monk by Lama Zopa Rinpoche in 1989, this gave way to my present duties as caretaker of the gompa, counselor, instructor, and retreat organizer. I received full ordination as a gelong in 1990 from His Holiness the Dalai Lama. Recently I have had to suspend most of my responsibilities to look after my aged mother who now suffers from Alzheimer's disease. She now lives with me at the Institute, and in taking care of her, I have to practice many things that I previously just pretended to practice.

At Vajrayogini Institute, I have had extraordinary opportunities to see and work with many people who, while looking for ways to make their lives meaningful, have turned toward the Buddha's teaching. It is for these voyagers, and all those who have the karma to have contact with this unworthy monk, that I would like to offer this meditation practice. I have found it useful as I try, falter, and try again to follow Buddha Shakyamuni's magnificent path of wisdom and bliss. Therefore, I offer it with the motivation of service and the hope that it might be of help to someone else wishing to pursue the path.

Institut Vajra Yogini
Lavaur, France

Tenzin Dasel
(Siliana Bosa)

I was conceived somewhere in Europe during my parents' six-month honeymoon, and I was born in South Africa in 1957. At the age of six, the whole family moved back to Italy. By the time I was twenty-two I felt I needed to take a break, to go off and have time to think and to take a rest from everything familiar. I was feeling that somewhere in the world there were beings who had the same feelings as I did, but I was not really clear about those feelings; nor was I able to express them. It was what the *I Ching* would describe as a "time to cross the great water." But I wasn't at all interested in any of the Asian religions that were newly spreading in the West.

Before deciding which destination to take for my future, I went to say goodbye to my sister, who was already living in Pomaia, at Istituto Lama Tsong Khapa. It was November 1979. The late Venerable Geshe Yeshe Tobten had just arrived from India and was giving teachings on a Lamrim text. These lasted all winter and spring. The first teaching I attended was incredible: it was just as if Geshe-la were talking about my life, explaining clearly all the thoughts I had never been able to express. After the third day of teachings, I went to see Geshe-la and asked him if I could take refuge. Then I never said goodbye, because I didn't need to run anywhere else. I could just stay there in front of Geshe Yeshe Tobten, drinking the nectar of his words, which were giving me the feeling of finally being nourished with the proper food. He has been the light that has dispelled a little of the obscuration in my life and given me the aspiration to let go of this constant up and down way of life. There at Pomaia I discovered the destination of my journey; I had already arrived. I was ready to start the great inner journey, the only one where you can find a true destination.

I became a resident at Istituto Lama Tsong Khapa, and for almost two years I received many incredible, precious teachings—which I really didn't understand at that time. These were given by many highly realized masters who have since passed away: Geshe Jampel Senge, Tsenshab Serkong Rinpoche, His Holiness Ling Rinpoche, and Lama Yeshe. When Geshe Yeshe Tobten went back to India after two years in Italy, I followed him to Dharamsala. He accompanied me when I went to receive ordination from His Holiness the Dalai Lama on April 18, 1981.

I am not really able to express the feelings that led me to that moment. Of course after more then eighteen years, it should be clear why I took such a step. Also, by now, it should be clear as well if what I thought was going to be true has actually been true or not. I can sincerely say that up to now I have never regretted taking ordination, mainly because I never blame it for my confused states of mind, which, as before, still arise. However, there is a small difference: I don't believe them anymore! This approach definitely helps a lot. With the passing years, I at least start to have more conviction about impermanence. Through experience I get closer to an understanding of life. That is already something!

I do not regret my decision to get ordained; I could even say I'm happy. But this does not mean I have any realizations. Deep in my heart there is a kind of satisfaction or contentment that gives me some confidence. In order to survive you have to accept your limits, and, even if you are not perfect in keeping your vows, you do what you can, rejoice about it, encourage yourself, and increase the aspiration to improve. I think the main practice of an ordained person is to try to constantly demonstrate kindness and a subdued manner in one's daily actions. I remember seeing a video of Lama Yeshe in which he said, "the purpose of being ordained is to be the servant of others." I felt such incredible joy just by hearing that. It really touched my heart, and I clearly remember that in that moment I expressed the wish to be able to develop such a dedicated mind.

I spent fourteen months in India, then went back to Instituto Lama Tsong Khapa. There I worked in the spiritual program department and helped organize the first tour of His Holiness the Dalai Lama to the FPMT centers in Europe. From 1988 to 1994 I was the director of

Centro Studi Cenresig in Bologna. During my stay I helped with the invitation and organization of two visits of His Holiness the Dalai Lama to my home city. I started *Siddhi,* one of the first Italian Buddhist magazines. Many times, I have been the interpreter for the teachings of His Holiness the Dalai Lama and Lama Zopa Rinpoche. Since 1998 I have lived in Nepal, first as the resident teacher at the Himalayan Buddhist Meditation Centre, then as the director.

Himalayan Buddhist Meditation Centre
Kathmandu, Nepal

Tenzin Dekyi
(Chantal Carrerot)

I was born in the south of France in 1954, the oldest of three daughters. My parents were Catholics from very religious families. Before marrying, my father had entered a seminary to become a priest but later abandoned this plan. Just before he died he told me that he always thought, "My children will do it." Of his three children, two of us have indeed taken robes. My middle sister became a Catholic nun around the same time that I took my first vows in 1986. Ten years later, she left her order and is presently a student of Buddhism.

As a child, I liked to go to church, but as I grew up, many questions began to haunt me. Why does everything exist? At times, I felt a sense of unreality. I studied psychology in Toulouse and received a Masters degree. Then I started to travel around Europe, but somehow I felt disoriented. My life was missing a purpose that I could not find in what was around me until I met the Buddha's teachings.

In 1983 I visited Institut Vajra Yogini to hear Geshe Sopa give a commentary on a text about the Buddhist view of reality. Immediately I felt connected to the Buddhist teachings, and I had to re-examine many of my previous beliefs. This teaching had a profound effect on my life, though I found it a bit difficult to integrate at first. There was then a community of nuns at the Institute, and of monks living at Nalanda Monastery. I was very impressed by the Sangha members. Often, in my dreams, in all kinds of situations, I would see robes. I recognized that Buddhism was bringing meaning to my life, and that taking ordination would give me the best conditions to follow the path. Being a nun would cut off unnecessary activities and involvements and allow me time and energy to study and practice Dharma. I had been longing to fully dedicate my life to a worthy project, and walking the path to liberation and helping others to do the same was more than I could have ever dreamed!

Although I wanted to be a nun and could see the benefits, taking vows for life seemed a huge commitment. I had followed an untamed and extravagant course of life for a few years and was used to it. Even though we want to move forward in our lives and on the path, we are often caught up in limiting patterns. We resist change and are afraid of extending ourselves. Apathy and dullness keep us where we are. What changed things for me was meeting Lama Thubten Zopa Rinpoche. The guru makes you extend yourself beyond your self-imposed limits, allowing you to bring about positive changes in your life.

In 1984, I started to live and work at Institut Vajra Yogini and to follow the study program at nearby Nalanda Monastery. I took temporary ordination for one year in 1985 and attended the Second Enlightened Experience Celebration in Nepal and India that winter. On the first of January 1986, along with seventy other women from the Himalayan regions and a few Westerners, I received novice vows in Bodhgaya from His Holiness the Dalai Lama. In 1992, in France, I took the vows of a fully ordained nun with the Venerable Thich Huyen Vi, abbot of the Vietnamese Linh Son Monastery, and the Venerable Geshe Tengye, resident teacher at Institut Vajra Yogini.

I have been much happier since I became a nun. The loss of my parents in a car accident in 1987 was a very painful experience, but it was also a strong inspiration to develop renunciation and an incentive to practice. For about eight years I studied at Nalanda Monastery. I had to live outside the monastery, sometimes with lay friends, but most of the time by myself or with other nuns. In those first years of ordination, the guidance and care I received from my teacher Geshe Jampa Tegchok—then Abbot of Nalanda—was very important. Besides taking advantage of all the profound teachings Geshe-la gave during those years, I also received sympathetic support. I believe this is very necessary during the first years after ordination.

After Geshe Tegchok was appointed Abbot of Sera Je Monastery in 1993, I lived mostly in India, at Sera and other places. From 1996, after some time in retreat, I worked as the spiritual program coordinator at Tushita Meditation Centre, Delhi, for over two years. Since 1998 I have been the director of the International Mahayana Institute. Now I am "homeless," traveling in response to opportunities to receive teachings, and to assignments to be carried out. My present assignment has taken me to Zimbabwe and South Africa to teach the Dharma, but I will return later this year to be the resident teacher at Kalachakra Centre in Paris.

Johannesburg, South Africa

Thubten Gyatso
(Adrian Feldman)

I was born in Melbourne, Australia, in 1943. My parents were both socialists, so I was brought up without any religion. My father had studied rabbinical philosophy and taught Hebrew at a Melbourne synagogue, but when he married my Christian mother, those activities came to an end. Science formed my worldview; however this began to fall apart when I took LSD (once) as a medical student.

In 1969 I finished medical school and immediately took the opportunity to indulge my wanderlust by working for a year as a junior doctor in a hospital in Papua New Guinea. Then I sailed as ship's doctor on a cargo ship from Melbourne to London. In England I earned a diploma in tropical medicine. London was still in its "swinging" stage, and I participated as much as I could in the psychedelic flower-power revolution. After two years this led me to Afghanistan, where my inner revolution continued, aided by a growing interest in Taoism and other things Eastern. Friends and I went down the Indus River in Pakistan in an eighteen-foot rowboat. That wonderful trip on the Indus changed me completely; I knew that whatever I was going to do in my life, it would not be "normal." Throughout those years I experienced the ups and downs of making and breaking relationships. Back in Australia, the sudden death of my mother created a huge challenge to my belief that I had control of my life. At the same time I began to receive letters from my friend Nick Ribush, who had discovered Kopan Monastery and was writing things about "sentient beings," which made me reach for the dictionary and wonder what had possessed his mind.

More than a dozen of his friends took the bait and attended the fourth meditation course at Kopan. I stayed home, believing salvation was in our own piece of land where we could live according to our own rules and opt out of society. Nick's response was, "its peace of mind you want, not piece of land." It took me six months to realize that he was right, but still I was not going to get into religion. The lady I was living with wanted to attend the sixth course at Kopan in March 1974, so I accompanied her to Bangkok, where I remained to look for work as a doctor. No suitable job was available, but one of the doctors who showed me around had been a Theravadin monk for three years. He was the first Western Buddhist I had met, and his calm demeanor impressed me. One night, on the hotel balcony in Chiang Mai, I took out Geshe Rabten's *The Graduated Path to Liberation,* a small book that Nick had sent me a year before that I had never read. I read it three times and immediately decided to go to Nepal for the course.

The course started with 250 Westerners, but after a week there were only 200, and then nearly 199. When I went to see Nick to tell him I couldn't stand it anymore, he looked up at me with big eyes and said, "But it's all true." "You've gotta be crazy," I thought, but decided to stick it out another week. Then precepts started, but not for me. Every morning I would sneak out of the tent and go down to Boudhanath for an omelet, toast, and porridge. After the course I had to go away and think about it. During one meditation I had realized that if I accepted karma and rebirth to be true, I would have to become a monk. To me, that was the obvious implication of the perfect human rebirth meditation. And the last thing I wanted to do in my life was to become a monk. So I set out to prove that the lamas were wrong about karma and rebirth.

Returning overland to Europe, I revisited familiar places in Pakistan and Afghanistan, this time seeing them through the eyes of Buddhism. In London all my friends were left-wing activists. I thought that perhaps anarchy was the solution to "society's woes"—I still believed problems were external. But in pubs and at parties, I realized I was arguing like Lama Zopa, "Can't you see that the fundamental problem is not the capitalist system but the anger and greed in our own minds?" The thought to return to India grew stronger. Lama Yeshe and Lama Zopa Rinpoche stood out beyond anybody else I had met in my life. I respected them and knew I could trust them. I had to go back to India and learn more about Buddhism.

After meditating with Goenka-Ji in Benares, I went Bodhgaya. Sitting under the Bodhi Tree, I finally decided to take refuge, which I did with Bero Khyentse Rinpoche, a young lama who spoke English. The next day I came down with malaria, so I returned to Australia. Lama Yeshe and Nick arrived in Melbourne soon after my return, and, at a five-day course near the seaside, I spoke to Lama Yeshe privately for the first time.

"Lama, I have taken refuge and want to practice Dharma as much as possible. I see two ways: one as a monk, the other with a partner, the two of us practicing together."

"Yes dear, it is possible to practice Dharma with a partner, but *very* difficult."

"Why?" I asked, defensively.

"Because, instead of just one crazy mind, you have two crazy minds," and he rolled over laughing for five minutes.

"Well," said I, still on the defensive, "What's the advantage of becoming a monk?"

"You can practice Dharma twenty-four hours a day," said Lama, and again collapsed into laughter—he had caught me because I had begun the conversation saying I wanted to practice Dharma as much as possible.

A week later, Lama Zopa Rinpoche and Lama Yeshe gave a Kopan-style one-month meditation course at Chenrezig Institute in Queensland, after which I knew I had to think deeply about Dharma. I built a cabin in the bush and retreated for three months, seeing nobody, following a strict daily schedule of precepts and meditation sessions, and reading Dharma books. Twenty-five years later I am still cruising on the wonderful energy of that retreat. Riding the crest of that feeling, I saw the futility of family life and took ordination as a monk at Kopan in November 1975. Since then I have had the great privilege to be always under the guidance of Lama Thubten Yeshe and Lama Thubten Zopa Rinpoche, and have had the opportunity to receive many teachings and do more retreats. I have helped establish Nalanda Monastery in France and Thubten Shedrup Ling Monastery in Australia, as well as FPMT centers in Nepal, Taiwan, and now, Mongolia.

Ganden Do Ngag Zung Juk Ling
Ulaan Bataar, Mongolia

Lobsang Tarchin
(Lorenzo Rossello)

I was born in Savona, northwest Italy, in 1951. I studied economics and commerce at the University of Turin and then worked at my father's company for seven years.

From a conventional point of view, there was nothing that I lacked: I had a good job and a good partner with whom I shared the same ideals and many interesting plans. But...I had a certain inner sensitivity that was pushing me to understand that what I was doing in my life was not meaningful. Maybe this was also because from the time I was a young child I had always felt a strong interest in and attraction to Eastern thought, especially to Tibetan Buddhism and Hinduism.

In short, my aspirations were mainly oriented toward ultimate truths rather than an ordinary and conventional life. Rather than asking myself "What will I do when I grow up?" I found more interesting the question "Who am I?" and "What meaning can be given to the life of a single individual?" I searched for possible answers in Western philosophy and psychology, in the Catholic religion, in Hinduism, and finally in Buddhism.

In Buddhism I found a resonance that was closest to my personality and my way of thinking. When I finally met a master who showed me that he had both the knowledge and capacity to realize in practice what he taught, I decided to take the last step and to become a monk. To pursue this goal I became a resident of Istituto Lama Tzong Khapa near Pisa in 1983. Five months later I formally took refuge and the five precepts of the lay practitioner from Venerable Geshe Jampa Gyatso, the resident teacher of the Institute.

On August 1, 1984, Geshe Jampa Gyatso conferred upon me the ordination of a novice monk and the spiritual name of Lobsang Tarchin.

Subsequently, on February 21, 1986, I received the full bhikshu (gelong) ordination in Dharamsala, India from His Holiness the Dalai Lama.

Since then, I have remained in Pomaia under the guidance of Geshe Jampa Gyatso. Thanks to his kindness I have succeeded both in giving some form to my spiritual longings and in integrating the meanings of his teachings. My life revolves around study, meditation, and the work and activities of the Dharma center.

Istituto Lama Tzong Khapa
Pomaia, Italy

Tenzin Dongak
(Fedor Stracke)

I was born in 1967 and grew up in Munich, Germany. In 1985 I became interested in Zen Buddhism during a time when I was trying to sort out my life. At that time in Germany, Tibetan Buddhism was not well known. But I did go to a public talk given by His Holiness the Dalai Lama. During that period I decided the only way to be happy was through meditation, and I tried to meditate every day. Since I had led a comparatively wild life for a few years I felt I had experienced enough of the world and could leave it behind. Even then I was playing with the idea of becoming a monk.

In 1986 I traveled overland to India with a vague idea of finding a guru and learning more about meditation and myself before getting caught up in the machinery of Western life. While in Pakistan I found it was possible for tourists to go into China via the Karakorum Highway. From there I would be able to go to Tibet, which, of course, held a certain fascination for me. I changed my plans, went to Tibet, and spent two and a half months there. I did not know much about Buddhism or the culture of the country, so when I first heard monks debating in Kumbum Monastery, I thought they were practicing some kind of Kung Fu! After seeing what they were up to, I still couldn't figure out what they were doing.

I circumambulated Tashi Lhunpo Monastery counterclockwise despite the admonitions from all the people coming around the other way. I guess I just wanted to be different. But I was really impressed with the devotion and practice of the Tibetan people. I thought, "If it is like this under the Chinese, then before the invasion it must have been truly awesome." By then I had encountered many different peoples and cultures, but I found the Tibetans by far the warmest. In Lhasa, somebody just coming from Nepal recommended Kopan Monastery as a place where you could stay cheaply and meditate. I think the "cheaply" part played a major role in my deciding to go to Kopan.

My first course was in early 1987 and was led by the Venerable David Marks. I decided then that the Lamrim system was the best explanation of the Buddhist path I had come across, so I stayed for five months trying to do a Lamrim retreat. During my retreat I made repeated dedications to be able to become a monk. I also tried to generate some renunciation as the basis for becoming a monk. I thought there could not possibly be anything more important in my life than inner development, and I wanted to dedicate my life to it. Afterward I went to India and attended teachings by His Holiness the Dalai Lama. During this time I decided I was still too young to become a monk. I thought I should experience more of the world first. I know now that this kind of thinking was just creating obstacles. I went back to Nepal for the November Course at Kopan that year. Hearing the Lamrim teachings again convinced me, so at the end of 1987 I took rabjung vows with Lama Zopa Rinpoche in Kopan. It was the beginning of ordained life for me.

In 1988, I took getsul ordination with His Holiness the Dalai Lama in Dharamsala and, in 1994, gelong ordination, also with His Holiness, at Sera Monastery. After my getsul ordination I stayed in India and Nepal for two years but felt it was fruitless to commute between Dharamsala and Kopan. I wanted to stay somewhere to study Buddhism in greater depth. Kirti Tsenshab Rinpoche advised me to go to Sera Monastery. I went to Europe and stayed at Nalanda Monastery in France for the seven months it took to get an Indian student visa. I returned to India in 1990, and in May formally entered Sera-Je Monastery, where I enrolled in the Geshe program. Following the study program is one of the best things I have done in my life. My class is now in its thirteenth year.

As well as my studies I have been involved in establishing a house for IMI monks studying at Sera-Je. It is called IMI House, and in 1996 I became its director. I have also taught and translated in FPMT centers in India, Nepal, Germany, New Zealand, and Australia. I was fortunate to be asked by Lama Zopa Rinpoche to teach the 1999 November Course at Kopan.

IMI House, Sera-Je Monastery
Bylakuppe, India

Thubten Tsultrim
(George Churinoff)

I was born in 1945 in Chicago in the United States. Being lazy by nature I didn't study much, but I was very fond of science. In 1967 I graduated with a B.S. in physics from the Massachusetts Institute of Technology, where I was a mediocre student, preferring to spend my time worrying about life rather than studying. After dropping out of Ph.D. studies I pretended to work for a while at MIT until finally escaping to live in Vermont. There I picked apples, tutored, read a lot about the Sufis and mysticism in general, and tried to decide what to do with my life. This led to a job teaching in Beirut, where I hoped to come in contact with the Sufis or at least to find a more satisfying philosophy of life than provided by our Western materialistic culture.

After finishing my contract in Beirut, I set out on an overland trip to India in the summer of 1974 to study yoga in its birthplace. In Kabul, I met two women who told me about a meditation course at Kopan Monastery taught by Lama Yeshe and Lama Zopa Rinpoche. From their description it seemed it was what I had always been looking for, so I immediately set out for Nepal and changed the course of my life.

On a train through India to Nepal, I saw a robed Indian being teased by some youths, who took away his walking staff. Ever the meddling teacher, I told them to give back the man's cane. One thing led to another, and I ended up with bruises, welts, and a well-dented ego. The boys escaped with the staff, while many people passively watched the spectacle. I reentered the train to meet an Indian ascetic sitting on the floor near the toilets and asked him in amazement: "Why?" The ascetic replied: "Karma!" I later felt the incident had been my first encounter with the guru.

After the seventh Kopan Course in November 1974, I stayed on for a couple of months to do the first organized Lamrim retreat along with a couple of dozen other intrepid souls (non-souls?). Afterward I traveled to Dharamsala to study at the Library of Tibetan Works and Archives for six months and then went back again to Kopan to do a Vajrasattva retreat.

During the next Kopan Course I decided to take ordination. A friend who was going to get ordained asked me if I was thinking about ordination. I said I thought I had some things to do first, which, at that time, meant having a meaningful relationship. He asked: "But, when will there be a better time?" and I recognized I might never encounter such a perfect situation again. I asked Lama Zopa Rinpoche's advice that evening and Rinpoche replied: "For you it would be very good." This indicated that ordination is not necessarily for everyone but that it would be good for me.

I took ordination as a novice in early 1976 and full ordination a year later. I remained in Nepal and India for more than four years to continue studying Tibetan Buddhism and to do several retreats at Kopan and in Dharamsala. Lama Yeshe then asked me to be the spiritual program coordinator at Manjushri Institute in England. I remained there over three years, studying in the general program as well as in the first FPMT Geshe Studies program.

Following that, for several years I served as spiritual program coordinator at Istituto Lama Tzong Khapa in Italy, escaping occasionally for retreats in India. At Lama Yeshe's request, I helped organize the Institute's first seven-year study program with Geshe Jampa Gyatso. It continues today under Geshe-la's guidance. Preparing for these courses, I translated several texts into English, including the *Autocommentary to the Madhyamakavatara,* the text used to study the subtle meaning of emptiness according to the highest philosophical view. After the second Enlightened Experience Celebration, Lama Zopa Rinpoche asked me to be the teacher at Tushita Meditation Centre in New Delhi. I continued my own studies for the next couple of years there and studied for sizable periods at Sera-Je Monastery in South India, the Tibetan Institute of Dialectics in Dharamsala, and the Institute of Higher Tibetan Studies at Sarnath. I was awarded an M.A. in Buddhist studies at the University of Delhi.

After another stay at Istituto Lama Tzong Khapa in Italy, I went to

Sera-Je Monastery for the teachings of His Holiness the Dalai Lama on the *Autocommentary to the Madhyamakavatara*. I had the opportunity to present a copy to His Holiness of my English translation of the text and also gave copies to all the Western participants. Lama Zopa Rinpoche requested that I be the English tutor to Lama Osel Rinpoche at Sera-Je. I lived there for about three and a half years, mainly teaching Lama Osel reading, writing, mathematics, and science but occasionally taking some courses of my own.

Since then, I have continued to study, meditate, and translate texts from Tibetan into English. I have taught around the world for extended periods in Russia, Mongolia, Singapore, Australia, and the United States.

Thubten Norbu Ling

Santa Fe, U.S.A.

Sangye Khadro
(Kathleen McDonald)

I was born in California in 1952. I was raised Roman Catholic, but in my early teens I decided I did not want to be a Catholic because I found some of its beliefs difficult to accept. I had a very inquisitive mind, however, and really wanted to know the answers to such questions as who or what is God, why are we here, what happens after we die, and why there is so much suffering and injustice in the world. In my later teens, through reading books, I came across Eastern religions and felt very comfortable with the ideas of reincarnation and karma. As a student at university, that interest developed through reading, learning yoga, and meeting fellow students who were practicing Buddhism. I felt strongly attracted to a contemplative way of life.

My interest became so strong that I decided to leave university and travel to India to search for spiritual teachers. I arrived in Dharamsala, India, in 1973, and stayed for five months studying Buddhism with Geshe Ngawang Dhargyey at the Tibetan Library. I was very attracted to the teachings on bodhichitta and emptiness. I also felt that the teachers and Tibetan people really practiced their beliefs—I was so impressed by their compassion, generosity, unselfishness, and amazing devotion and dedication to their religion. Their example really inspired me. During this time I also met Lama Thubten Yeshe and Lama Thubten Zopa Rinpoche, who came to Dharamsala to visit their retreat center, Tushita.

I left Dharamsala at the end of 1973 because I was not able to renew my visa. I headed for Nepal, stopping in Bodhgaya along the way to attend the Kalachakra initiation given by His Holiness the Dalai Lama. In Nepal I stayed at Kopan Monastery and attended classes along with twelve or so Western monks and nuns who had recently been ordained in Bodhgaya. It was around this time that I began thinking seriously about getting ordained myself. I had never been interested in the usual things like getting married, raising kids, developing a career, making money, and buying things; but I just did not know what I *did* want to do with my life until I met Buddhism. I was deeply inspired by Buddhist teachings—especially bodhichitta—and by the lamas who were so compassionate, wise, renounced, and dedicated to a life of contemplation and benefiting others. I felt that there was nothing I wanted to do with my life other than practice the Dharma, and being a nun would provide the best situation to do that. Seeing Westerners who had become monks and nuns strengthened my feeling that there could be no better way of using my life than to dedicate it to learning Buddha's teachings, practicing them, and sharing them with others.

During the one-month Lamrim course at Kopan in the spring of 1974, this idea grew even stronger as I listened to Lama Zopa Rinpoche talk again and again about the faults of the eight worldly dharmas and the importance of renunciation. I requested ordination from the lamas, and in May, Zong Rinpoche, a very high lama from Ganden Monastery and guru to both Lama Yeshe and Lama Zopa Rinpoche, ordained me.

I stayed in Nepal for the next three years studying and doing retreat; afterward I returned to America. Since then I have lived in various FPMT centers, studying and doing retreat when I can, but mainly teaching, as that is what Rinpoche has always asked me to do. I have been in Singapore for the last ten years, where I have learned a lot about devotion and generosity from the local Chinese people. Of course it is not an easy way of life—but there is no easy life in samsara! Whatever lifestyle you choose will have its good and bad sides. I think it's up to each person to choose the way of life—ordained or lay—that best suits. I am happy to be ordained; it really does provides the best situation for me to be able to spend my life learning and practicing the Dharma. There are also many opportunities for helping others—for example, teaching and counseling—which, in turn, are helpful for my own spiritual growth.

Amitabha Buddhist Centre
Singapore

Jamyang Wangmo
(Helly Pelaez Bozzi)

I was born in Spain in 1945. I studied in Granada University and obtained a degree in law. I never really liked it, so I decided to enter art school and follow my natural inclination toward art. My emotional and affective life was a big mess, and after a couple of years I decided to give up everything and go to India in search of a "wise man" who could teach me how to change my mind and how to make my life useful. After one year of traveling through Greece and five months in India, I returned to Spain totally convinced that I had to devote my life to the spiritual path, although I wasn't sure about which path I had to follow.

In 1972 I went back to India and then to Nepal. There I met Lama Thubten Yeshe and Lama Thubten Zopa Rinpoche, and I did a one-month meditation course with Lama Zopa Rinpoche. These teachings changed my life, and before the end of the course I had already decided to become a nun. Then I met His Holiness the Dalai Lama in Bodhgaya, did another meditation course, and went to Dharamsala to ask Lama Yeshe for ordination. After being ordained by Geshe Rabten, I spent most of my time in the mountains in the Solo Khumbu region of Nepal, doing solitary retreats. After three years I was asked by Lama Zopa to paint a Chenrezig tangka for Lawudo Gompa. Afterward Lama Yeshe asked me to paint a large Tara tangka and to teach painting to the monks and Westerners staying at Kopan Monastery. I also started to translate Tibetan texts at the request of Lama Yeshe.

In 1987 I realized that being a novice nun for the rest of my life did not make much sense. After all, every monastic community has novices and fully ordained members, and I could not see any reason why after so many years of being a novice I could not become a full member of the Buddhist Sangha. I received permission from His Holiness the Dalai Lama and Lama Zopa Rinpoche to take full ordination as a bhikshuni.

I contacted Polin Monastery in Hong Kong, and, thanks to Karma Lekshe Tsomo (an American nun who had already taken the bhikshuni ordination), I was able to take full ordination there in November 1987. The next year I attended the first dual ordination that took place in Hsi Lai Temple in Los Angeles.

Since then I have lived mainly in Dharamsala, inspired by the compassionate energy of His Holiness, where I do retreats and work on books and translations. So, that's my life. Most of my ordained life I have been known as Jampa Chökyi, but recently I have begun to use Jamyang Wangmo, a name I received many years ago.

Tushita Meditation Centre
Dharamsala, India

Thubten Kunsel
(Robina Courtin)

When I was little, I decided at Mass that I wanted to be a priest. I must have been very little, because when everyone laughed and explained that I couldn't be, I simply didn't understand the logic: it was clear that it was my job. Reluctantly I accepted, and decided to be a nun instead. When I was twelve, I begged my mother, on bended knees, to let me be a Carmelite like my great hero St. Thérèse of Lisieux. I cried when she said no.

Twenty years later, she cried when I told her I planned to be a nun after all—a Buddhist nun. "I wish I'd let you be a nun when you wanted to be!" she said.

Clearly my connection with monasticism runs deep. And my twelve years at Sacre Cœur, a Catholic convent in Melbourne, where I was born and raised, played a big part in this. Because I was rebellious and proud, I had a hard time at school, but I am forever grateful for the emphasis on the importance of morality and integrity: this education gave me the infrastructure of my life.

A seven-inch LP of Billie Holliday—"I wonder who 'he' is?" I thought—bought for sixpence at the school fete when I was fifteen opened me up to a whole new world: my spiritual aspirations began to take on social and political dimensions. When I was nineteen I gave up God, happily choosing boys and drugs instead.

My mother persuaded me to continue my classical singing education (she'd been my teacher for ten years) in London when I was twenty-three. But it was 1967 and I was ready and ripe for revolution. A hippy first, I was soon working full time in radical left politics. I really found my political identity as a feminist and, back in Melbourne in 1972, was part of the burgeoning movement there.

By the time I was thirty, after eight intensive years of trying to bash the world into the shape I thought it should be, I began to look for something spiritual again. It was clear that I'd have to stop hating the rest of the human race. When I was a hippy, I blamed straight people for the suffering in the world; as a communist I blamed the rich; as a defender of blacks, I blamed whites; and as a feminist, I blamed men. There was no one left but me.

I went back to Mass and tried various types of meditation, but they didn't fit. In 1976, after a couple of years of martial arts, I landed at a course on Buddhism at Chenrezig Institute in Queensland given by Lama Yeshe and Lama Zopa Rinpoche. I'd come home! By now, I'd given up sex, drugs, alcohol, and cigarettes, so the logical next step was to be a nun—finally! Eighteen months later I took ordination at Kopan Monastery in Kathmandu.

For the first ten years I worked for Wisdom Publications. As editor of an international Buddhist magazine, *Mandala,* since 1996, I'd receive letters from people in prison interested in studying Buddhism. That activity has grown into Liberation Prison Project, which takes care of the spiritual needs of hundreds of inmates in the United States, many on death row or with life sentences. And we've started the project in Australia as well.

The inmates are a huge inspiration to me: people with nothing good in their lives, and nothing to look forward to, having the courage to find themselves and learn to give to others—the job I'm attempting to do, too.

Liberation Prison Project
Taos, New Mexico, U.S.A.

Glossary

afflictive emotion (Sanskrit: *klesha*) A thought that is in its nature suffering and gives rise to suffering. Other synonyms are delusion, disturbing thought, fettering passion, and disturbing emotion. The three principal afflictions are ignorance, attachment, and anger, or aversion.

Amitayus The "Buddha of Infinite Life" and an aspect of Buddha Amitabha, the "Buddha of Infinite Light."

arya A Sanskrit term meaning noble and used in Buddhism to indicate someone who has directly realized emptiness, the true nature of all existence.

Asanga The fourth-century Indian pandit who received directly from Maitreya Buddha the extensive, or method, lineage of Shakyamuni Buddha's teachings. His writings are the basis for the Mind-only school of Buddhist tenets.

Atisha (982–1054) The renowned Indian Buddhist master who came to Tibet to help revive Buddhism, spending the last seventeen years of his life there. Lama Atisha wrote the first Lamrim text, *Lamp on the Path to Enlightenment,* and founded the tradition of the Kadampas, practitioners renowned for their renunciation and bodhichitta.

attachment The afflictive emotion that exaggerates the pleasant aspect of something, simply because it appears to make one feel happy and secure. It also conceives the object as being permanent and acts to create an obsession with, and dependence on, that object.

aversion Afflictive emotion that projects negative qualities on its object.

bhikshu/bhikshuni Fully ordained member of the Buddhist Sangha.

Bodhgaya The place of Shakyamuni Buddha's enlightenment. Now a small town in Bihar State, northern India. Representatives of virtually every traditional form of Buddhism have established temples and meditation centers there.

bodhichitta Literally, "mind of enlightenment." The mind wishing to achieve enlightenment in order to be able to benefit all living beings. It is synonymous with *bodhi mind*.

bodhi mind See *bodhichitta*.

bodhisattva Someone who has generated bodhichitta.

Boudhanath A district on the outskirts of Kathmandu, Nepal, where one of the holiest Buddhist stupas is located.

buddha An enlightened being.

Buddhadharma See *Dharma*.

buddhahood See *enlightenment*.

buddha nature or *buddha potential* The capacity of the mind to achieve full enlightenment.

cause and effect The law that all impermanent phenomena, both material and mental, arise and pass away in dependence on primary causes and coordinating conditions. See also *karma*.

calm abiding (Skt. *shamata*) A type of meditative practice for developing effortless single-pointed concentration.

chakra The subtle energy centers of the body of which the most important are those at the crown, throat, and heart.

Chenrezig (Skt. *Avalokiteshvara*) A buddha symbolizing or embodying enlightened compassion.

clear light The very subtle level of mind that is obscured by afflictive emotions and gross conceptualization; also refers to the object, emptiness, of the clear light mind.

compassion The wish that another being may be free of mental and/or physical suffering.

conqueror Synonym for *buddha*.

craving See *attachment*.

cyclic existence (Skt. *samsara*) Existence controlled by delusion and karma, which is by nature unsatisfactory and suffering. Human existence is one of six possible kinds of existence in the desire realm. Other realms include the form and formless realms, where beings experience a sublime existence. One never remains permanently in any of these realms, but cycles from one to another according to karma. The purpose of Buddhist practice is to eliminate the causes of cyclic existence to achieve liberation and enlightenment.

death process The gradual absorption, or dissolution, of the physical and mental faculties of a person that occurs naturally at death. Each of the eight stages of the death process is accompanied by an inner sign, or vision. The first four visions, which accompany the absorption of the four elements and the five senses, are a shimmering mirage, smoke, sparks or fireflies, and flickering flame. The second four visions are experienced as white light, red light, blackness or darkness, and clear light.

deity (Tib. *yidam*) The tantric aspect of a buddha, visualized to help develop specific qualities.

deity practice The tantric practice of generating oneself in the form of a meditational deity within purified surroundings and reciting the sadhana of that deity.

delusion See *afflictive emotion.*

dependent arising Relative; interdependent. The way that the self and all phenomena exist conventionally: they come into being in dependence upon 1) causes and conditions, 2) their parts, and, mostly subtly, 3) the mind imputing or labeling them.

Dharamsala A hill-station town in the state of Himachal Pradesh, India. It includes the Tibetan-dominated village of McLeod Ganj, where His Holiness the Dalai Lama lives. Tushita Retreat Centre, started by Lama Yeshe, is located in the hills above the village.

Dharma The teachings of the Buddha that lead to liberation and enlightenment.

dharmakaya The omniscient mind of a buddha that is able to directly perceive all phenomena of the past, present, and future while simultaneously perceiving both their conventional and ultimate natures.

disturbing attitude. See *afflictive emotion.*

Dorje Pagmo A wrathful tantric female deity, red in color, used for transforming desire. An aspect of Vajrayogini.

eight Mahayana precepts Eight purificatory vows taken by lay people for a duration of twenty-four hours.

eight worldly dharmas The worldly concerns that generally motivate the actions of ordinary beings: 1) being happy when acquiring something; 2) being unhappy when not acquiring something; 3) wanting to be happy; 4) not wanting to be unhappy; 5) wanting to hear interesting sounds; 6) not wanting to hear uninteresting sounds; 7) wanting praise; 8) not wanting criticism. [Sometimes 5) and 6) are explained as wanting fame and not wanting notoriety, respectively. (Pabongka Rinpoche, *Liberation in the Palm of Your Hand*, p. 335.)]

emptiness (Skt. *shunyata*) Refers to the ultimate nature of phenomena, which is that they are empty of an inherently existing self-nature. Also called voidness. Synonymous with selflessness.

Enlightened Experience Celebration Special FPMT events held in India and Nepal. The first, organized by Lama Yeshe, took place between late 1981 and mid-1982 so that Lama's students could receive teachings and initiations from the most important Gelugpa lamas. A second was held in 1985–86 and the third in 1990.

enlightenment Buddhahood; awakening. The final goal of the Buddhist path and the potential of all sentient beings, enlightenment is achieved when all obscurations are removed from the mind and one has developed both omniscience and infinite compassion for all beings.

equanimity The mind that has impartial feeling for all beings, not labeling them as friend, enemy, or stranger.

field of merit (also *refuge field*) The enlightened beings one visualizes at the beginning of deity practice as a basis for taking refuge.

four noble truths The first teaching given by the Buddha: the truth of suffering, the true cause of suffering, the true cessation of suffering, the true path to the cessation of suffering.

five aggregates (Skt. *skandha*) Five components of a person, the physical form plus four mental components of feeling, recognition, consciousness, and compositional factors.

five elements Earth, water, fire, air, and space.

five precepts The basic level of ethical conduct for a lay Buddhist. The five precepts are abstaining from taking life, from taking what is not offered, from saying what is not true, from sexual misconduct, and from taking intoxicants.

four continents. In Buddhist cosmology, the four lands that surround Mount Meru. Humans live on the southern continent of Jambudvipa.

FPMT The Foundation for the Preservation of the Mahayana Tradition.

gelong/gelongma See *bhikshu/bhikshuni.*

Gelug One of the four schools of Tibetan Buddhism. Founded by Lama Tsongkhapa in the fifteenth century. The last of the four schools of Buddhism to develop in Tibet.

geshe Someone who has completed the extensive study program and passed examinations at one of the Gelug monastic universities.

getsul Buddhist monk or nun with novice ordination vows.

Goenka-ji A well-known meditation master who trained in Burma and teaches a form of Theravada Buddhism.

gompa Tibetan term used to refer to a monastery or temple.

Graduated Path (Tib. *Lamrim*) The presentation of all the Buddha's teachings in a concise form showing how to train the mind step by step to achieve enlightenment. First developed by Lama Atisha in his *Lamp on the Path to Enlightenment* and later elaborated on extensively by masters of the Gelug school.

guru Literally, "heavy" [with knowledge]. A spiritual teacher; a lama. Mahayana Buddhism, especially the tantras, emphasizes the importance of having a qualified guru to lead one to enlightenment.

guru-buddha A meditational deity that one visualizes as a manifestation of one's guru.

guru devotion The fundamental tantric practice, whereby one's guru is seen as identical with the buddhas, one's personal meditational deity, and the Three Jewels.

hell/hell beings The samsaric realm of the greatest suffering. A being who inhabits that realm. *See also* lower realms.

Hinayana Literally, the Lesser Vehicle. The path of the arhats, the goal of which is nirvana, or personal liberation from samsara.

hungry ghost (Skt. *preta*) One of the six class of samsaric beings, hungry ghosts experience the greatest sufferings of craving, especially hunger and thirst. *See also* lower realms

ignorance The root affliction that gives rise to all other afflictions. It is the root cause of all suffering. Its eradication is the goal of the Hinayana path. In the Mahayana path, one first has to eliminate ignorance to advance along the path to enlightenment. Also called self-grasping.

initiation A tantric ritual conducted by a qualified lama that enables the student to engage in tantric deity practice.

Kalachakra A tantric deity. The practice associated with this deity can lead to complete enlightenment, even in one lifetime.

karma The actions of body, speech, and mind; the imprints in the mind created by those actions; and the results of the ripening of those imprints. See also *cause and effect.*

King of Prayers A very popular prayer of dedication to the bodhisattva way of life associated with the bodhisattva Samantabhadra; taken from the *Avatamsaka Sutra.*

Kopan Monastery Founded by Lama Thubten Zopa Rinpoche and Lama Yeshe and located twenty minutes from Boudhanath Stupa near Kathmandu, Nepal. Originally started as a center for teaching Tibetan Buddhism to foreigners, it now includes a monastery with 300 Tibetan and Nepalese monks and a nunnery with 250 nuns. Courses for foreigners are given monthly, culminating each year with the month-long November Course.

Kyabje Ling Rinpoche Senior tutor to His Holiness the Dalai Lama and the ninety-sixth Ganden throne holder, the title bestowed on the head of the Gelug school of Tibetan Buddhism. He died in 1983.

Kyabje Trijang Rinpoche Junior tutor of His Holiness the Dalai Lama and the root guru of Lama Yeshe and Lama Zopa Rinpoche. He died in 1981.

lama See *guru.*

Lamrim See *Graduated Path.*

liberation The state of being irreversibly freed from all suffering and its causes. It is synonymous with *nirvana*.

lower realms The three realms of cyclic existence with the greatest suffering: hell realm, realm of the hungry ghosts, and animal realm.

Madhyamaka The Middle Way philosophy propounded by the great bodhisattva Nagarjuna (ca. 200 A.D.), which reveals the definitive view of the Buddha's teaching on emptiness.

Mahamudra Literally "the great seal" in Sanskrit; refers to the ultimate nature of the mind, emptiness, and the wisdom consciousness experiencing that emptiness.

Mahayana The "great vehicle" of the bodhisattvas that leads to enlightenment. It emphasizes that beyond achieving our own liberation, we have to help all other beings to be free of suffering and to achieve complete happiness.

mandala offering The symbolic offering to the Buddha of the entire purified universe.

Manjushri The deity embodying all the buddhas' wisdom.

mantra Literally, "protection of the mind." The mind is protected from ordinary appearances and conceptions, and from seeing oneself and other phenomena as mundane. Also refers to Sanskrit syllables recited in conjunction with the practice of a particularly meditational deity that embody the qualities of that deity.

merit The positive energy accumulated in the mind as a result of virtuous actions of body, speech, and mind.

mind Defined as that which is mere clarity and knowing. Although formless, it is the basis of all existence and all experience. It is not the brain or any product of the brain; synonymous with consciousness.

mindfulness An awareness of the moral state of one's mind—the nature of the thoughts arising moment by moment—whether they are beneficial or not for one's spiritual well-being, combined with a willingness to skillfully oppose what is harmful and strengthen what is beneficial.

mindstream Synonymous with mind, but emphasizing that mind is arising moment by moment in a beginningless and endless stream of experience; awareness; consciousness.

Mt. Meru In Buddhist cosmology, this giant mountain at the center of the universe is the abode of the two lowest classes of gods of the desire realm.

Namgyalma (Skt. *Ushnishavijaya*) Tantric deity whose meditation practice can extend the lifespan and help overcome obstacles to Dharma practice.

nirvana The state of definite liberation from all suffering and its causes. The final goal of the Hinayana, or individual vehicle.

November Course Also called the Kopan Course. A month-long meditation course on the Graduated Path to enlightenment. It has been held annually at Kopan Monastery since 1971. Originally Lama Thubten Zopa Rinpoche taught the whole course with Lama Yeshe giving some talks. It was through these courses that many Westerners connected with the lamas and, due to their inspiration, went home to start Dharma centers. This is the way the FPMT began. Since the late 1980s the courses have been taught mainly by senior Western students of the lamas, with Lama Zopa Rinpoche teaching during the last ten days.

obscurations There are two kinds of obscurations that cloud the mind: the *knowledge obscurations* are the afflictions that prevent liberation; and the *obstacles to omniscience* are subtle imprints of the afflictions that prevent enlightenment.

perfect human rebirth The rare human state, qualified by the eight freedoms and the ten richnesses, which is the ideal condition for practicing Dharma and attaining enlightenment.

potentials Positive and negative karmic imprints. These imprints have the potential to ripen as happiness or suffering respectively. Also referred to as karmic seeds.

precepts Various levels of vows; some can be taken for just a day others are for life. There are lay precepts and precepts of the ordained Sangha. Taking vows or precepts involves avoiding certain negative actions, and, by so doing, greater positive potentials are created than by avoiding these actions without the precepts. On the other hand, breaking the precepts creates greater negative potential than doing the negative action without the precept.

prostrations Ritual bowing that is done to pay respect to the Three Jewels. It is also done to purify negative karma and especially the delusion of pride. There is a traditional practice of doing one hundred thousand prostrations to prepare the mind for tantric practice.

rabjung vows Preliminary ordination vows.

refuge Reliance upon Buddha, Dharma, and Sangha in order to overcome suffering and achieve enlightenment.

renunciation The attitude of wishing to be free from suffering—either that of this life or of all of cyclic existence. In the first case one seeks to work for a better rebirth. In the second, one seeks liberation from cyclic existence in order to achieve either nirvana or enlightenment.

retreat Doing more intensive meditation and or other spiritual exercises while avoiding normal worldly activities; usually done in a quiet, isolated, natural setting.

root guru One's main spiritual teacher or guide. This is the teacher one feels closest to and whom one trusts to lead one to liberation and enlightenment.

sadhana The method of tantric meditation, or the text outlining this process. Each deity practice has its own sadhana.

Samantabhadra The primordial buddha understood as the ultimate source of the Buddhist tradition.

samsara See *cyclic existence.*

Sangha The community of ordained followers of the Buddha. The arya Sangha are those who have attained direct insight into the true nature of existence and, therefore, constitute the actual Sangha refuge.

self-cherishing A negative mind that arises from ignorance or self-grasping and tries to protect and reinforce the sense of self through following the afflictions, believing that they will bring happiness.

selflessness See *emptiness.*

Shakyamuni Buddha (563–483 B.C.) The historical Buddha who was born into the Shakya clan, the fourth of the one thousand founding buddhas of this present world age.

six perfections The practices of a bodhisattva based on bodhichitta. They are generosity, morality, patience, enthusiastic perseverance, concentration, and wisdom.

six realms of samsara See *cyclic existence.*

six root disturbing attitudes or emotions The main afflictions from which all other disturbing thoughts arise. They are ignorance, attachment, anger, pride, doubt, and wrong views. See also *afflictive emotions.*

special insight (Skt. *vipashyana*) Direct experience of the way things actually exist. *See also* emptiness

stupa Reliquary representing the mind of the Buddha.

suffering (Skt. *dukkha*) There are three levels of suffering. The first level is obvious physical and mental pain or discomfort. The second, more subtle level is called changeable suffering, which ordinary beings believe to be happiness but which is unfulfilling and frustrating because it does not last. The most subtle level is called compounded pervasive suffering, which refers to our existential condition of having a body and mind produced and controlled by affliction and karma and ensnared in cyclic existence.

sutra Scripture recording the words of the Buddha.

Sutrayana The non-tantric vehicle of Buddhism as outlined in the Hinayana and Mahayana sutras.

tangka Tibetan name for a religious scroll painting.

tantra The esoteric aspect of the Mahayana. It is the fastest method to achieve enlightenment.

Tara The female buddha symbolizing the enlightened activities of all buddhas.

Three Jewels The Buddha, Dharma, and Sangha. Refuge in the Three Jewels is the threshold of Buddhist practice.

Tibetan Library (In full: The Library of Tibetan Works and Archives.) Established by His Holiness the Dalai Lama in Dharamsala as a research institute and place where non-Tibetans can study Tibetan Buddhism.

Theravada The form of Buddhism dominant in Southeast Asia, which emphasizes achieving one's own liberation.

Tsongkhapa 1357–1419. The founder of the Gelug school. One of his disciples became the first Dalai Lama.

Uttaratantra A Mahayana text taught by Maitreya Buddha to Asanga. It explains how all sentient beings possess buddha nature.

Vairochana A buddha who symbolizes the pure body of a buddha. The aspect assumed by the Buddha when he taught the tantras.

Vajrasattva Male meditational deity symbolizing the purity of all buddhas. Vajrasattva practice purifies past negative actions and removes obstacles to Dharma practice.

Vajrayana The tantric path of Buddhism, which allows the practitioner to attain enlightenment in a single lifetime.

Vajrayogini A female tantric deity of the highest class of tantra embodying blissful wisdom.

Vinaya The rules of training observed by members of the Sangha. It is also the group of teachings explaining this code of behavior.

vipassana The Pali word for *vipashyana,* which means "special insight." The vipassana retreats offered by students of Goenkaji involve ten days of silent sitting meditation and meditation on the four foundations of mindfulness. In Tibetan Buddhism, *vipashyana* usually refers to insight into the ultimate truth of emptiness.

voidness See *emptiness.*

wisdom One of the two wings (with compassion) of the Mahayana path, and the last of the six perfections. In this context, it refers to the purified consciousness arising at an advanced stage of the path that directly perceives the empty nature of existence.

Further Reading

TRADITIONAL

Pabongka Rinpoche. *Liberation in the Palm of Your Hand*. Michael Richards, trans., Boston: Wisdom, 1991.

Tsong-kha-pa. *The Great Treatise on the Stages of the Path to Enlightenment: Lam Rim Chen Mo*. Joshua W. C. Cutler and Guy Newland, eds., Ithaca, NY: Snow Lion, 2000.

Yeshe Tsondru. *The Essence of Nectar*. Geshe Losang Tharchin, Benjamin and Deborah Alterman, trans., Dharamsala: Library of Tibetan Works and Archives, 1979.

MODERN

Batchelor, Martine. *Meditation for Life*. Boston: Wisdom, 2001.

Chodron, Thubten. *Buddhism for Beginners*. Ithaca: Snow Lion, 2001.

Gunaratana, Henepola. *Mindfulness In Plain English*. Boston: Wisdom, 1993.

Johnson, Will. *The Posture of Meditation: A Practical Manual for Meditators of All Traditions*. Boston: Shambhala, 1996.

Khema, Ayya. *Being Nobody, Going Nowhere: Meditations on the Buddhist Path*. Boston: Wisdom, 1987.

Loden, Geshe Acharya Thubten. *Meditations on the Path to Enlightenment*. Melbourne: Tushita, 1996.

McDonald, Kathleen. *How to Meditate: A Practical Guide*. Boston: Wisdom, 1986.

Rabten, Geshe. *The Essential Nectar: Meditations on the Buddhist Path.* London: Wisdom, 1984.

Rabten, Geshe and Geshe Ngawang Dhargyey. *Advice from a Spiritual Friend.* Boston: Wisdom, 2001.

Sopa, Geshe Lhudrub. *Peacock in the Poison Grove: Two Buddhist Texts on Training the Mind.* Boston: Wisdom, 2001.

Tenzin Gyatso, H. H. the Dalai Lama. *Cultivating a Daily Meditation.* Dharamsala: Library of Tibetan Works and Archives, 1991.

Valham, Karin. *Lam-Rim Outlines: Beginners' Meditation Guide.* Boston: Wisdom Publications and Kopan Monastery, 1997.

Wallace, B. Alan. *Tibetan Buddhism from the Ground Up.* Boston: Wisdom, 1994.

Wangchen, Geshe Namgyal. *Awakening the Mind: Basic Buddhist Meditations.* Boston: Wisdom, 1995.

Yeshe, Lama. *Introduction to Tantra: The Transformation of Desire.* Boston: Wisdom, 2001.

Yeshe, Lama and Lama Zopa Rinpoche. *Wisdom Energy: Basic Buddhist Teachings.* Boston: Wisdom, 2000.

Zopa Rinpoche, Lama. *A Daily Meditation Practice: How to Meditate on the Graded Path to Enlightenment.* Boston: Wisdom, 1997.

———. *The Door to Satisfaction: Heart Advice of a Tibetan Buddhist Master.* Boston: Wisdom, 2002.

———. *Transforming Problems into Happiness.* Boston: Wisdom, 2001.

The Foundation for the Preservation of the Mahayana Tradition

The Foundation for the Preservation of the Mahayana Tradition (FPMT) was founded in 1975 by Lama Thubten Yeshe as a nonprofit organization devoted to the worldwide transmission of the Mahayana Buddhist tradition and values through teaching, meditation, and community service. They provide integrated education through which people, inspired by an attitude of universal responsibility, can develop the highest potential of their minds for the benefit of others. They are committed to creating harmonious environments and helping all beings develop their full potential of infinite wisdom and compassion. They do this through meditation, study, and retreat centers—both urban and rural—monasteries, publishing houses, healing centers, and other related activities. At present, there are more than 130 FPMT activities in twenty-four countries worldwide.

The basis of this work is the Mahayana Buddhist teachings as presented in the Tibetan Gelug tradition—founded in the fifteenth century by the great scholar, yogi, and saint, Lama Tsongkhapa—and particularly as taught by our founder, Lama Yeshe, and Spiritual Director, Lama Thubten Zopa Rinpoche.

Every three months, the Foundation publishes *Mandala* magazine from its International Office in the United States. For more information about the organization, please contact:

FPMT International Office
125B La Posta Road, Taos, NM 87571, USA
Telephone: 1-505-7587766; fax: 1-505-758-7765;

Email: fpmtinfo@fpmt.org
or check out our website at www.fpmt.org

Our website also offers teachings by His Holiness the Dalai Lama, Lama Yeshe, Lama Zopa Rinpoche, and many other highly respected teachers in the tradition. You can also find details about the FPMT's educational programs; a complete listing of FPMT centers all over the world and in your area; and links to FPMT centers on the Web with details of their programs, and to other interesting Buddhist and Tibetan home pages.

Lama Thubten Yeshe

 Lama Thubten Yeshe was born in Tibet in 1935. At the age of six, he entered the great Sera Monastic University in Lhasa, where he studied until 1959, when the circumstances surrounding the Tibetan uprising against the Chinese invasion of Tibet forced him into exile in India.

Lama Yeshe continued to study and meditate in India until 1967, when with his chief disciple, Lama Thubten Zopa Rinpoche, he went to Nepal. Two years later he established Kopan Monastery, near Kathmandu, in order to teach Buddhism to Westerners.

In 1974, the Lamas began making annual teaching tours to the West, and as a result of these travels, a worldwide network of Buddhist teaching and meditation centers—the Foundation for the Preservation of the Mahayana Tradition—began to develop.

In 1984, after an intense decade of imparting a wide variety of incredible teachings and establishing one FPMT activity after another, at the age of forty-nine, Lama Yeshe passed away. He was reborn as Osel Hita Torres in Spain in 1985 and was recognized as the incarnation of Lama Yeshe by His Holiness the Dalai Lama in 1986.

As the monk Lama Tenzin Osel Rinpoche, he is studying for his geshe degree at Sera Je Monastery, one of the great Tibetan monastic universities now reestablished in South India. Lama's remarkable story is told in Vicki Mackenzie's book, *Reincarnation: The Boy Lama* (Wisdom Publications, 1996).

Some of Lama Yeshe's teachings have been published by Wisdom Publications. The books include *Wisdom Energy, Introduction to Tantra, The Tantric Path of Purification,* and *The Bliss of Inner Fire.* These are available through FPMT centers or at www.wisdompubs.org.

Other short works by Lama Yeshe have been produced for free distribution by Lama Yeshe Wisdom Archive. These include *Becoming*

Your Own Therapist, Advice for Monks and Nuns, and *Make Your Mind an Ocean.* Lama Yeshe may also be seen on videotape: *Introduction to Tantra, The Three Principal Aspects of the Path,* and *Offering Tsok to Heruka Vajrasattva* are available from the Lama Yeshe Wisdom Archive. See their website, www.LamaYeshe.com.

Lama Thubten Zopa Rinpoche

 Lama Thubten Zopa Rinpoche was born in Thami, Nepal, in 1945. At the age of three he was recognized as the reincarnation of the Lawudo Lama, who had spent the last thirty years of his life meditating in a nearby cave known as Lawudo, within sight of Rinpoche's Thami home. Rinpoche's own description of his early years may be found in his book, *The Door to Satisfaction* (Wisdom Publications).

At the age of twelve, Rinpoche went to Tibet and studied and meditated at Domo Geshe Rinpoche's monastery near Pagri, until the circumstances surrounding the Tibetan uprising against the Chinese occupation of Tibet in 1959 forced him to forsake Tibet for the safety of India. Rinpoche then went to the Tibetan refugee camp at Buxa Duar, West Bengal, India, where he met Lama Yeshe, who became his closest teacher.

The lamas went to Nepal in 1967 and over the next few years built Kopan and Lawudo Monasteries. In 1971 Lama Zopa Rinpoche gave the first of his famous annual Lamrim retreat courses, which continue at Kopan to this day.

In 1974, with Lama Yeshe, Rinpoche began traveling the world to teach and establish centers of Dharma. When Lama Yeshe passed away in 1984, Rinpoche took over as spiritual head of the FPMT, which has continued to flourish under his peerless leadership. More details of Rinpoche's life and work may be found on the FPMT website, www.fpmt.org. Rinpoche's other published teachings include *Wisdom Energy* (with Lama Yeshe), *Transforming Problems into Happiness, Ultimate Healing*, and a number of transcripts and practice booklets (available from Wisdom at www.wisdompubs.org).

Other short works by Lama Zopa Rinpoche have been produced for free distribution by the Lama Yeshe Wisdom Archive. These include *Virtue and Reality, Making Life Meaningful,* and *Teachings from the Vajrasattva Retreat.* See their website, www.LamaYeshe.com.

The International Mahayana Institute

The International Mahayana Institute is the community of monks and nuns of the FPMT. Its purpose is to support the Sangha in many ways—financially, educationally, and by providing an environment conducive for its members to maintain their ordinations. In this way, the IMI encourages the growth of future generations of Sangha, which in turn helps Buddhism remain a living tradition worldwide. The Buddha said, "Wherever there is Sangha, there the Dharma will flourish." He also said, "Wherever a monk or nun observes the Vinaya, that place is luminous. I myself abide there."

Lama Yeshe established the IMI in 1973 for the benefit of non-Tibetan monks and nuns. For the first few years it was based at Kopan Monastery. But with the spread of the FPMT to many countries there are now more than seven IMI monastic communities, and the total membership exceeds 220 monks and nuns from many Western countries, the Chinese-speaking world, as well as many other countries. Most are living in monastic communities or Dharma centers where they study, teach, meditate, and serve others in general, while preserving their ordination and the Buddhist monastic tradition. Lama Thubten Zopa Rinpoche is the abbot of the IMI as well as the spiritual director of the FPMT.

Adopting the life of a renunciate is a lifelong commitment in the Tibetan Buddhist tradition. One takes ordination because one realizes that this human life really is rare and precious and wants to use it in the most meaningful way—both for oneself and others—and to set up one's life to have the conditions for practicing Dharma full time. Essentially, one takes vows in order to live in a disciplined way, free from distractions to following the path to liberation and enlightenment. Since the Sangha are freed from many of the distractions that go with an ordinary working and family life, they have more time to engage in intensive study and practice. To be able to live this life the Sangha have always depended on the support of lay people. In return they are able to repay this kindness by teaching and giving guidance and inspiration. There is a great need for well-trained Sangha from all nations. The world needs monks and nuns who have done the studies and retreats necessary to present the Dharma effectively and who can provide inspiration to others from their own culture. It is much easier, and perhaps more important, for these people to present the Dharma to their peers, especially at the introductory level. Such monks and nuns serve as a bridge bringing Dharma newcomers up to the level where they can take teachings from Tibetan teachers who have studied the Buddhadharma extensively for many years. It is essential to the future of the Buddha's teachings that, eventually, Sangha of all nations become qualified to teach at the most advanced levels.

The IMI has established the Lama Yeshe Sangha Fund (LYSF), which, with the support of generous benefactors, is helping IMI Sangha become properly qualified to teach and serve sentient beings. At present, the Fund can support only a few of the IMI's members who have no other financial resources or benefactors. Each is given between $150 and $200 monthly to cover their minimal needs for food and shelter while engaged in study or retreat. Meanwhile, many other monks and nuns are left to solve their material problems on their own. This can often lead to difficulties. Financial stress makes it hard to maintain one's ordination correctly. If adequate funds were available, many more monks and nuns would be able to keep their ordinations purely and remain focused on becoming qualified teachers in order to serve sentient beings. We would also be able to meet the material needs of the IMI Sangha, provide facilities for basic and advanced study and retreat and, later, care and medical treatment for elderly Sangha.

Therefore, we need to dramatically increase the size of the LYSF. We need your help. By making it possible for monks and nuns to study and meditate you have a unique opportunity to create special merit. Benefactors will also receive the yearly IMI Sangha magazine and in appreciation of your support, IMI Sangha will make regular prayers for your health, happiness, and all success in accordance with the holy Dharma. Lama Zopa Rinpoche has said, "Even after death, whoever donates to this fund will get the merit of having contributed, for as long as the Sangha continues to exist."

If you would like to help the Lama Yeshe Sangha Fund you can send a donation to:

FPMT International Office
125B La Posta Road, Taos, NM 87571, USA
Telephone: 1-505-758-7766
Fax: 1-505-758-7765 • Email: fpmtinfo@fpmt.org

Payments can be made by check payable to the FPMT (in $US only). Please note on your check that it is for the Lama Yeshe Sangha Fund. You may make a monthly pledge or a one-time donation. Payment can also be made by Visa, MasterCard, or American Express credit card.

It is also possible to make online donations through the IMI website: www.fpmt.org/IMI. In the United States, all donations are tax-deductible.

IMI Communities

NALANDA MONASTERY
Rouzegas Labastide St-Georges,
Lavaur 81500 France
Director: Ven. Jean-Francois
Bergevin
Tel: (33) 05 63 58 02 25
Fax: (33) 05 63 58 19 87
Email: nalanda@compuserve.com
Website: www.ourworld.compu-
serve.com/homepages/nalanda

TAKDEN SHEDRUP TARGYE LING
MONASTERY
c/o Instituto Lama Tzong Khapa,
Via Poggiberna 9
56040 Pomaia (Pisa), Italy
Manager: Ven. Thubten Tsognyi
Tel: (39) 050 68 56 54
Fax: (39) 050 68 57 68
Email: iltk@libero.it
Website: www.padmanet.com/iltk

THUBTEN SHEDRUP LING
MONASTERY
RMB 1530, Eaglehawk, Victoria
3556, Australia
Director: Ven. Tony Beaumont
Tel/fax: (61) 03 5446 3691
Email: tsl@impulse.net.au
Website: www.shedrupling-
monastery.org

CHENREZIG NUNS COMMUNITY
c/o Chenrezig Institute, PO Box 41
Eudlo, Queensland, Australia
Manager: Ven. Yeshe Khadro
Tel: (61) 07 5445 0077
Fax: (61) 07 5445 0088
Email: chenrezig@ozemail.com.au

SHENPHEN SAMTEN LING
NUNNERY
c/o Instituto Lama Tzong Khapa,
Via Poggiberna 9
56040 Pomaia (Pisa), Italy
Tel: (39) 050 68 56 54
Fax: (39) 050 68 57 68
Email: iltk@libero.it
Website: www.padmanet.com/iltk

JINSUI FARLIN SANGHA
COMMUNITY
c/o Jinsui Farlin
F12-1, No 81, Section 3
Pa-Te Road, Taipei, Taiwan
Director: Ven. Choying Sangmo
Tel: (886) 02 2577 0333
Fax: (886) 02 2577 0510
Email: jinsuifa@ms3.hinet.net

SHEDRUP ZUNG DREL LING
(IMI HOUSE)
Sera-Je Monastery, House #3
PO Bylakuppe, Mysore
Karnataka 571104, India

Director: Ven. Fedor Stracke
Email: seraimihouse@yahoo.com
Website: www.seraimihouse.org

TUSHITA SANGHA COMMUNITY
c/o Tushita Meditation Centre
McLeod Ganj, Dharamsala
Kangra District, HP 176 219 India
Tel: (91) 1892 21866
Fax: (91) 1892 21246 Attn:
    Tushita
Email: tushita@ndf.vsnl.net.in
Website: www.come.to/tushita

NUNS HOUSE
c/o Tse Chen Ling
4 Joost Ave
San Francisco CA 94131 USA
Tel: 1 (415) 333-3261
Fax: 1 (415) 333-4851
Email: tclcenter@aol.com
Website: www.tsechenling.com

KACHOE ZUNG JUK LING ABBEY
3071 176th Street
Surrey, BC V4P 3C4 Canada
Director: Ven. Ann McNeil
Tel/fax: 1 (604) 541-8797
Email: anilaannmcneil@compu-
serve.com

If you would like to make a specific donation to any of these communities, it can be done through the FPMT International Office. See details on page 155. Please indicate for which community the donation is intended.

For further details or information about the IMI and its communities and activities, please contact the director of the IMI, Ven. Chantal Carrerot at: chantalcar@compuserve.com

Care of Dharma Books

The Buddhadharma is the true source of happiness for all sentient beings. Books like this show you how to put the teachings into practice and integrate them into your life whereby you get the happiness you seek. Therefore, anything containing Dharma teachings or the names of your teachers is more precious than other material objects and should be treated with respect.

These are but a few considerations to avoid creating the karma of not meeting the Dharma again in future lives. Please do not put books (or other holy objects) on the floor or underneath other things; do not step over or sit upon them; do not use them for mundane purposes such as propping up wobbly tables. They should be kept in a clean, high place, separate from worldly writings, and wrapped in cloth when being carried around.

Should you need to get rid of Dharma materials, please do not throw them in the rubbish but burn them in a special way. Briefly: Incinerate such materials alone—not with other trash—and as they burn, recite the mantra OM AH HUM. As the smoke rises, visualize it pervading all of space, carrying the essence of the Dharma to all sentient beings in the six samsaric realms, purifying their minds, alleviating their suffering, and bringing them all happiness, up to and including enlightenment. Some people might find this practice a bit unusual, but it is given according to tradition. Thank you very much for your consideration.

About Wisdom

WISDOM PUBLICATIONS, a not-for-profit organization, is dedicated to making available authentic Buddhist works for the benefit of all. We publish translations of the sutras and tantras, commentaries and teachings of past and contemporary Buddhist masters, and works by the world's leading Buddhist scholars. We publish our titles with the appreciation of Buddhism as a living philosophy and with the special commitment to preserve and transmit important works from all the major Buddhist traditions.

To learn more about Wisdom, or to browse our books online, please visit our website at wisdompubs.org. If you would like to receive a mail-order catalog, please contact us at:

Wisdom Publications
199 Elm Street
Somerville, Massachusetts 02144 USA
Telephone: (617) 776-7416 • Fax: (617) 776-7841
Email: info@wisdompubs.org • www.wisdompubs.org

Wisdom Publications is a non-profit, charitable 501(c)(3) organization affiliated with the Foundation for the Preservation of the Mahayana Tradition.